CW00495386

REVISE PEARSON EDEXCEL G

History

MEDICINE IN BRITAIN, c1250–present

PRACTICE PAPER Plus+

Series Consultant: Harry Smith

Author: Kirsty Taylor

This Practice Paper is designed to complement your revision and to help you prepare for the exam. It does not include all the content and skills you need for the complete course and has been written to help you practise what you have learned. It may not be representative of a real exam paper. Remember that the official Pearson specification and associated assessment guidance materials are the only authoritative source of information and you should always refer to them for definitive guidance.

For further information, go to: **quals.pearson.com/GCSEHistory**

Pearson

Published by Pearson Education Limited, 80 Strand, London, WC2R 0RL.

www.pearsonschoolsandfecolleges.co.uk

Copies of official specifications for all Pearson qualifications may be found on the website: qualifications.pearson.com

Typeset, produced and illustrated by QBS Learning
Cover illustration by Eoin Coveney

First published 2020

23 22 21 20

10 9 8 7 6 5 4 3 2 1

British Library Cataloguing in Publication Data

A catalogue record for this book is available from the British Library

ISBN 978 1 292 31016 9

Printed in Slovakia by Neografia

Acknowledgements

Content written by Ben Armstrong is included.

Text Credits:

P13, 29, 30, Boolarong Press: Extract from Diaries of a stretcher-bearer 1916–1918 (Ed. Donald Munro). Edward Charles Munro. Boolarong Press (2010), 26; **P61, 64, 66 Amberley Publishing Limited:** Extract from Eyewitness accounts: Diary of a nursing sister (2014). Anon © Amberley Publishing. **P17 Pearson Education Ltd:** Pearson Edexcel Level 1/Level 2 GCSE (9–1) in History – Specification – Issue 2 – December 2018 © Pearson Education Limited 2018; **P43 Pearson Education Ltd:** Pearson Edexcel Level 1/ Level 2 GCSE (9–1) in History – Sample Assessment Materials (Question Papers) – Issue 2 – July 2019 © Pearson Education Limited 2019

Photo Credits:

123RF: Johan2011 23, **Getty Images:** John Warwick Brooke/Hulton Archive 13, Popperfoto 61.

Notes from the publisher

1. While the publishers have made every attempt to ensure that advice on the qualification and its assessment is accurate, the official specification and associated assessment guidance materials are the only authoritative source of information and should always be referred to for definitive guidance. Pearson examiners have not contributed to any sections in this resource relevant to examination papers for which they have responsibility.

2. Pearson has robust editorial processes, including answer and fact checks, to ensure the accuracy of the content in this publication, and every effort is made to ensure this publication is free of errors. We are, however, only human, and occasionally errors do occur. Pearson is not liable for any misunderstandings that arise as a result of errors in this publication, but it is our priority to ensure that the content is accurate. If you spot an error, please do contact us at resourcescorrections@pearson.com so we can make sure it is corrected.

Contents

About this book

This book is designed to help you prepare for your Pearson Edexcel GCSE (9–1) History Medicine in Britain, c1250–present exam. It focuses on the skills you will need to answer the exam questions successfully.

You could work through the book in order. Alternatively, you could go straight to the section you want to focus on.

This Practice Paper Plus book

1 Knowledge booster
- ✓ Get started with these quick, warm-up activities
- ✓ Recap what you already know about the topic
- ✓ Find out what you need to revise in more detail
- ✓ Use the links to the Revise Pearson Edexcel GCSE (9–1) History Revision Guide and Workbook to find more revision support

2 Exam skills
- ✓ Get useful tips and guidance on how the exam works and what you need to do
- ✓ Understand how each question type works
- ✓ See how to write a successful answer with the 'steps to success' skills builders
- ✓ Learn how to avoid common mistakes

3 Practice paper
- ✓ Write straight into this book
- ✓ Have a go at a full practice paper on this topic
- ✓ Use the hints and reminders in the margins to stay focused on what you need to do to answer each question successfully
- ✓ Tackle the paper under exam conditions by covering up the guidance in the margins

4 Practice paper answers
- ✓ Read the mark schemes and notes to find out what a successful answer would include
- ✓ See full example answers to each question
- ✓ Look at the annotations and comments to understand what makes each answer successful
- ✓ Get ideas about how to improve your own responses in the exam

Knowledge booster

The Middle Ages

This key topic is about medicine in medieval England from c1250 to c1500. It covers ideas about the cause of disease and illness, and approaches to prevention and treatment, in this period.

Supernatural and religious explanations for disease

1 Decide which statements are true and which are false. Circle your answers.

A.	The Church dominated medieval society.	True	False
B.	People believed the placement of planets and stars caused disease.	True	False
C.	The Church encouraged people to search for the causes of disease.	True	False
D.	The Church approved of the ideas of Galen because he was a Christian.	True	False
E.	Most people believed God caused disease because he was angry with them.	True	False
F.	The Church ran universities where physicians were trained.	True	False

Rational explanations for disease

2 Complete the table below explaining the Theory of the Four Humours.

blood	Spring	Air	Hot and wet
Yellow bile	Summer	fire	
Black bile	Autumn	Earth	
phelgm	Winter	wate	Cold and wet

3 (a) Name the Ancient Greek doctor who created the Theory of the Four Humours.

~~Galen~~/ Hippocrates

(b) Name the Greek doctor who developed the Theory of the Four Humours.

Galen

4 Name Galen's theory which aimed to balance a patient's humours.

theories of opposite

5 What is the name of the rule that was written by Hippocrates, and which is still used today, where all doctors swear to respect life and prevent harm?

the hippocratic oath

6 Name **two** common methods Galen and Hippocrates used to prevent and treat disease.

- purging
- bleeding

7 Define the term **miasma**.

bad air (rotting organic matter).

The Middle Ages

Approaches to prevention and treatment

8 Complete the table below. Circle the correct options in the 'Training' and 'Costs' columns. Then add **two** examples to each row in the final column.

	Training	Costs	Examples of services they provided
Physicians	None Some University	Fairly cheap Expensive	Diagnose illness.
Apothecaries	None Some University	Fairly cheap Expensive	
Barber surgeons	None Some University	Fairly cheap Expensive	

9 Draw lines to match the type of treatments on the left with the examples on the right.

A. Rational	**i.** Praying, fasting, going on pilgrimage
B. Supernatural	**ii.** Bleeding and purging
C. Religious	**iii.** Hanging a magpie's beak round your neck

10 Name one **main** purpose of hospitals in this period. ....

The Black Death

11 Add **at least three** more ideas to this concept map.

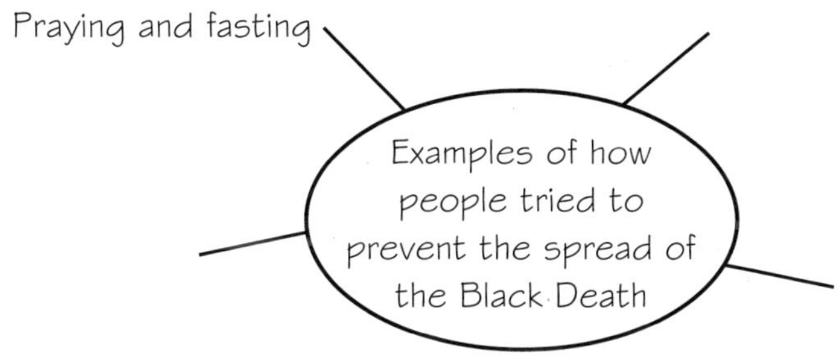

Revision Guide

How did you do? Go to pages 1–5 of the Revision Guide to remind yourself of any points you aren't sure about, and for more about this key topic.

Knowledge booster

The Renaissance

This key topic is about the Medical Renaissance in England from c1500 to c1700. It covers ideas about the cause of disease and illness, and approaches to prevention and treatment, in this period.

Ideas about the cause of disease and illness

1 In the period c1500–c1700, some ideas about what caused disease were largely the same as they had been in the Middle Ages. List **two** examples of ideas that stayed the same.

- ....
- ....

2 Fill in the gaps to complete this explanation of how ideas about the cause of disease changed during the Renaissance. Use some of these words: accepted; challenged; declined; diagnosing; increased; rational; still believed; stopped believing; treating.

During the Renaissance, people .... old ideas. This included religious ideas. Most people .... in God but the authority of the Church .... Fewer people .... that God caused disease and people started to look for new, ... ideas instead. Gradually there was a new scientific approach to .... illness.

3 Tick (✓) the correct answers.

(a) Thomas Sydenham was an important doctor because:

A. he treated the symptoms of a disease after carefully observing patients. ☐

B. he used a scientific approach when diagnosing and treating patients. ☐

C. he promoted the new Germ Theory, recently published by Louis Pasteur. ☐

(b) The printing press was important in medicine because:

A. it meant that new ideas were written down for the first time. ☐

B. it meant that all doctors had access to the same books to diagnose and treat patients. ☐

C. the ideas of scientists and doctors were shared more quickly and across a wider area. ☐

(c) The Royal Society helped to change medicine by:

A. helping scientists' ideas be shared, confirmed or dismissed, and giving money to fund research. ☐

B. publishing a journal called *Philosophical Transactions*. ☐

C. making sure all doctors were trained in the same way, using the same theories and texts. ☐

The Renaissance

Approaches to prevention and treatment

4 Which of the following is the best description of how physicians' training changed during the Renaissance? Tick (✓) the correct answer.

A. There was no real change – physicians were still trained at universities run by the Church. ☐

B. There was gradual change as universities had a wider range of books, and training began to include practical experience. ☐

C. There was great change as training moved away completely from textbooks to practical experience. ☐

William Harvey

5 Use some of these words to complete the description of the work of Harvey: the Church; dissection; Galen; heart; Hippocrates; liver; medical schools; physician; surgeon; Vesalius.

William Harvey proved that .... was right and that blood flowed towards the heart. This proved that .... was wrong. Harvey discovered that blood was pumped around the body by the .... He was a royal .... so his work was widely read. By 1700 it was being taught in .... His methods of observation and .... were copied by others who wanted to find out more.

The Great Plague, 1665

6 Some of the treatments and methods of prevention used during the Great Plague (1665) were similar to the ones used in the Black Death (1348–49). Other treatments and methods of prevention were different. Add **two** examples to each column below.

Similarities	Differences
• Sufferers and their families were quarantined	• Great Plague: Sufferers were wrapped up and put by fires to try to sweat disease out

Revision Guide

How did you do? Go to pages 6–11 of the Revision Guide to remind yourself of any points you aren't sure about, and for more about this key topic.

Knowledge booster

18th and 19th centuries

This key topic is about medicine in England from c1700 to c1900. It covers ideas about the cause of disease and illness, and approaches to prevention and treatment, in this period.

Germ Theory and why it was important

1 Put these events in order. Write numbers in the boxes.

☐ **A.** Robert Koch proved that microbes cause disease.

☐ **B.** Louis Pasteur proved that a weakened version of a microbe created immunity to the disease.

☐ **C.** Louis Pasteur published his Germ Theory, theorising that microbes in the air cause disease.

☐ **D.** Other scientists created vaccines for some human diseases.

☐ **E.** Robert Koch developed an easier way of growing bacteria and discovered that chemical dyes stain bacteria.

☐ **F.** Robert Koch identified the specific microbe that caused TB.

☐ **G.** Louis Pasteur discovered that microbes in the air cause decay.

☐ **H.** Louis Pasteur created a vaccine for chicken cholera.

Approaches to prevention and treatment

2 Add **at least two** examples to this concept map.

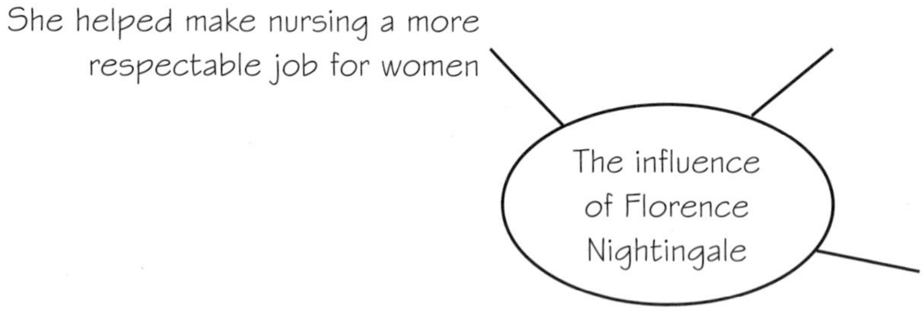

3 Complete the following paragraph to describe the impact Simpson and Lister had on surgery. Use some of these words: anaesthetic; antiseptic; aseptic; carbolic spray; chloroform; infection; surgery.

James Simpson discovered that .... was an effective .... Joseph Lister discovered that .... was an effective .... He inspired others to search for methods to prevent .... which led to .... conditions for surgery by 1900.

18th and 19th centuries

Jenner and vaccination

4 Decide which statements are true and which are false. Circle your answers.

A.	Jenner discovered why cowpox gave people immunity to smallpox.	True	False
B.	The Royal Society helped spread Jenner's ideas.	True	False
C.	Jenner published his findings himself.	True	False
D.	Vaccination against smallpox quickly became popular in Britain.	True	False
E.	Jenner's methods were used to find vaccinations to other diseases.	True	False
F.	Few people opposed Jenner because his ideas worked.	True	False

Fighting cholera in London

5 Tick (✓) the correct answers.

(a) When were there serious outbreaks of cholera in London?

A. 1831–32, 1848–49 and 1853–54 ☐ **C.** 1831–32, 1853–54 and 1860–61 ☐

B. 1825–26, 1848–49 and 1860–61 ☐ **D.** 1825–26, 1848–49 and 1853–54 ☐

(b) During which outbreak did John Snow begin studying cholera?

A. 1825–26 ☐ **B.** 1831–32 ☐ **C.** 1848–49 ☐ **D.** 1860–61 ☐

(c) In 1854, John Snow mapped deaths from cholera in which part of London?

A. Bethnal Green ☐ **B.** Mayfair ☐ **C.** Soho ☐ **D.** Whitechapel ☐

(d) Where was the water pump that Snow linked to the cholera deaths?

A. Broad Street ☐ **B.** Greek Street ☐ **C.** Harley Street ☐ **D.** Market Street ☐

(e) How did Snow show this water pump was spreading cholera?

A. He found the microbe causing cholera in the water from the pump. ☐

B. He had the pump destroyed. ☐

C. He removed the handle so people couldn't collect water from the pump. ☐

D. He found a leaking cess pit was next to the water pump. ☐

(f) Which of the following was an **immediate** impact of John Snow's work?

A. A new sewer system was built in London. ☐

B. A Public Health Act forced authorities to provide clean water. ☐

C. The cholera outbreak in Soho stopped. ☐

D. He proved the Germ Theory. ☐

Revision Guide

How did you do? Go to pages 12–17 of the Revision Guide to remind yourself of any points you aren't sure about, and for more about this key topic.

Modern Britain

This key topic is about medicine in Britain from c1900 to the present day. It covers ideas about the cause of disease and illness, and approaches to prevention and treatment, in this period.

Ideas about the cause of disease

1 Answer the following questions on discoveries in the field of genetics.

(a) Which scientists worked on building the first model of DNA? ....

(b) Whose x-ray photographs were used to help build a model of DNA?

....

(c) What is the name of the structure of DNA discovered in 1953? ....

(d) What is the name of the project which began in 1990 to identify and map every gene in human DNA? ....

2 Draw lines to match the lifestyle factors on the left with the negative impacts on health on the right.

A. Smoking	**i.** Liver disease, kidney disease, many cancers
B. Drinking alcohol	**ii.** Emphysema, heart disease, many cancers
C. Poor diet	**iii.** Heart disease, diabetes, many cancers

Improvements in diagnosis and treatment

3 Add **two** more examples to each column in the table.

Technology used in diagnosis since 1900	Technology used in treatment since 1900
• MRI, CT and ultrasound scans	• Dialysis machines

New approaches to prevention

4 Fill in the gaps to complete the description of new approaches to prevention in the 20th and 21st centuries. Use some of these words: cures; health; lifestyle; NHS; research; vaccinations; tetanus; measles.

Since the creation of the .... in 1946, the UK government has funded more medical .... to find more ways to prevent disease. It also funds .... to prevent people contracting diseases such as polio and .... There have been laws to improve .... and safety at work and reduce pollution. The government has also funded .... campaigns to raise awareness of dangers to health and encourage healthy behaviour.

Knowledge booster

Modern Britain

Advances in medicines

5 Answer the following questions about 20th-century treatments.

(a) What is the name given to a chemical compound that targets and kills a microbe causing a specific disease? ....

(b) What name is given to a drug which destroys or prevents the growth of bacteria?

....

(c) What disease were Paul Ehrlich and his team trying to find a cure for in the early 20th century?

....

(d) What was the first antibiotic? ....

(e) Give **one** example of an illness treated with Prontosil. ....

The development of penicillin

6 Complete this timeline about the key events in the development of penicillin.

- **1928** Alexander Fleming discovers that mould kills bacteria.
- **1929** ....
- **1939** ....
- **1940** ....
- **1941** US drug companies agree to fund Florey and Chain's research after UK companies would not. Florey and Chain prove that penicillin effectively kills infection in humans.
- **1942** ....
- **1943** British drug companies begin mass production of penicillin.

The fight against lung cancer

7 Give **two** examples of how the UK government has tried to prevent people from developing lung cancer as a result of smoking.

- ....
- ....

Revision Guide

How did you do? Go to pages 18–23 of the Revision Guide to remind yourself of any points you aren't sure about, and for more about this key topic.

Knowledge booster

The Western Front

The historic environment for this thematic study is the British sector of the Western Front, 1914–18. It covers injuries, treatment and the trenches.

Battles on the Western Front

1 Give the correct dates (month/s and year) for the following battles.

(a) First Battle of Ypres:.....................

(b) Battle on Hill 60:.....................

(c) Second Battle of Ypres:.....................

(d) The Somme:.....................

(e) Arras:.....................

(f) Third Battle of Ypres:.....................

(g) Cambrai:.....................

The trench system

2 Name **two** parts of the trench system.

- ....
- ....

Illness and injury at the Western Front

3 Complete the table below.

	Cause	Symptoms	Example of prevention method
Trench fever			
Trench foot			

4 **(a)** What caused most injuries and deaths?

....

(b) Name **two** types of bacteria in the soil which caused wound infection.

- ....
- ....

(c) Name **two** symptoms of gas attacks.

- ....
- ....

Knowledge booster

The Western Front

Chain of evacuation

5 Name the **two** organisations that provided most of the medical care on the Western Front.

- ....
- ....

6 What kind of treatment was given at Regimental Aid Posts? ....

7 Where were casualty clearing stations located? ....

Medical advances on the Western Front

8 Complete the table. Add **at least one** point to each empty cell.

	Situation pre-1914	Situation during war	Impact of war: advances made
Preventing and dealing with infection	Antiseptic, then aseptic, surgery was established to prevent infection during surgery and other procedures		
X-rays		Huge numbers of bullet and shrapnel injuries meant x-ray machines were essential for effective surgery	
Blood loss	• Human-to-human blood transfusions tried but often unsuccessful • Blood groups discovered in 1901		

Revision Guide

How did you do? Go to pages 24–28 of the Revision Guide to remind yourself of any points you aren't sure about, and for more about this key topic.

In the exam

After all your revision and preparation, you want to do well. There are some key things you should remember in the exam.

What should I take with me?

- You must write in **black**, so it is a good idea to have more than one black pen with you.
- You might want a highlighter to mark the key words in the questions.
- Don't fill your desk with loads of other things – you know you won't need a calculator, for example, so leave it in your bag.
- Don't bother with correction fluid – just cross out any mistakes.

Where should I start?

Start with the front cover of your exam paper.

- The most important bit is the space for your name – don't forget to write it!
- It tells you how much time you have for the exam.
- For Paper 1, it will remind you about the separate Sources Booklet – make sure you have this.
- It will tell you which questions you must answer, and which ones you can choose.

How can I stay focused?

1. Take deep, slow breaths at the start of the exam and to help you focus as you work through the paper.
2. Highlight the key words in the questions, like dates, to make sure you focus on the right thing.
3. Plan your answers, especially for the longer essay questions. Work out what you want to say before you start writing.
4. If you get stuck, try a new question and come back to the other one later. Or make a list of what you do know about the topic in the question to help you get started.

How can I manage my time?

- It is a good idea to divide your time. Spend more time on questions that are worth more marks. You could even write on the paper (on the front cover or next to each question) the time you will start each question before you begin answering.
- Check the time regularly to make sure that you still have enough time for the longer answers.
- If you haven't finished answering a low-mark question but you are running out of time, move on to a higher-mark question. You can come back if you need to.

How much should I write?

- Your exam paper will give you space to write in for each question.
- Use the number of marks as a guide to how much you should write – a 12-mark question will need more than a 4-mark one.
- You don't always need to fill the space – this does not necessarily mean more marks.

How should I check my work?

- Leave about five minutes at the end for checking.
- Check that you didn't miss any questions.
- Check your spelling and punctuation.
- Check that you have not made any obvious mistakes, like using the wrong date.

Top tip

If you run out of space to finish an answer, **ask for more paper**. Don't use the answer space for the next question – this will make your answer hard to read. If you use extra paper, write 'answer on extra paper' at the bottom of the answer space. Then write the question number on the extra paper and complete your answer. At the end, check any extra paper has your name on it and that it is clear which answers you have finished there.

Had a look ☐ Nearly there ☐ Nailed it! ☐

Writing clear answers

The most important thing in the exam is writing down the correct information, but it also helps to write clear, well-organised answers. This will make your answers easier to follow.

Get the basics right

- ✓ Use a good, **black** pen.
- ✓ Use paragraphs – they will help to make your points clearer.
- ✓ Write in the correct answer spaces. If you use extra paper, add a label to the new page to make it clear which question you are continuing. Write 'answer on extra paper' where you ran out of space.
- ✓ If you make a mistake, cross it out neatly.

How can I write clearly?

1. Always write in Standard English – formal language, not slang.
2. Use adverbials or linking phrases to connect ideas and make your meaning clear – such as 'for example', 'however', 'therefore', 'as a result', 'consequently', 'in addition', 'significantly', 'in contrast', 'similarly'.
3. Use key terms for the topic.

Does my handwriting matter?

Your work will be marked, no matter what your handwriting is like. **However**, it is always a good idea to write as neatly as you can to make sure all the words in your answer are clear.

Imagine you had to mark these sentences. Which is easiest to read?

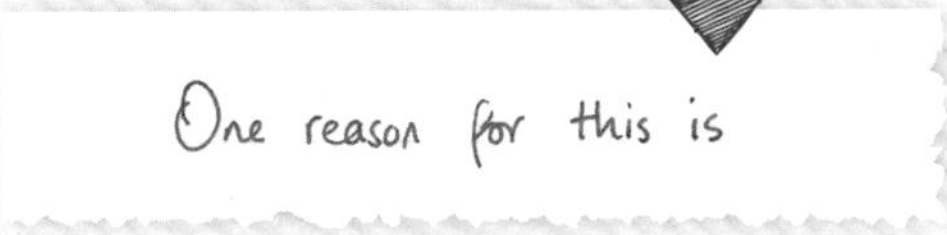

Should I plan my answers?

Top tip

Plans help you to organise your ideas.

- ✗ 4-mark questions – you don't need a plan for these short answers.
- ✓ 8-mark questions – you might find it helpful to jot down a quick plan, such as a short list of points to include.
- ✓ 12-mark and 16-mark questions – make a plan. Many of the best exam answers for these questions have plans.

There are different ways to plan. You can see examples on pages 25, 37 and 41.

How can I write effective paragraphs?

A good way to write effective paragraphs is to use **PEEL – Point, Evidence, Explain, Link:**

POINT – say what the paragraph is about.

EVIDENCE – give examples.

EXPLAIN – say what the evidence shows.

LINK – connect back to the question. This paragraph is answering the question 'Explain why the treatment of disease changed very slowly in the years c1500–c1700'.

> One reason that the treatment of disease changed very slowly during the Renaissance was that the new ideas and understanding of them did not affect treatment. For example, Andreas Vesalius dissected a large number of human bodies, and his detailed drawings were published in England and throughout Europe. This helped surgeons but not apothecaries and physicians. As a result, it was still difficult to diagnose and treat diseases. This meant that treatments stayed more or less the same.

Had a look ☐ **Nearly there** ☐ **Nailed it!** ☐

Working with sources

You need to know how to look at sources and how to work with them in the exam.

What is a source?

A source is a piece of historical evidence from the time period you are looking at.

Top tip

When you read or examine a source, look for three things:

- What is the source about?
- Is there an opinion or a message in the source?
- Does the source agree with or challenge what you know about the topic?

What sources are in the exam?

- There will be two sources. You will find them in a separate Sources Booklet.
- At least one of the sources will be a written source (like a diary entry or a speech). The other could be a written source or an image (like a poster or a photograph).
- They will be connected to your study of the historic environment, the British sector of the Western Front, 1914–18: injuries, treatment and the trenches.

Analysing the content of a source

Source A: A photograph of stretcher bearers at the Third Battle of Ypres, August 1917, taken by Lieutenant John Brooke, an official British army photographer on the Western Front.

About: Getting the wounded off the battlefield.

Message: Conditions made transporting the wounded difficult.

Agrees with what I know: Ypres ground conditions were awful due to bad weather.

Source B: An extract from the diary of Lance Corporal Edward Munro of the Army Medical Corps, dated 25 August 1916. He was a stretcher bearer on the Western Front.

> Some of the 7th Field Ambulance bearers had to carry … near the front line … While I was watching them a shell burst nearby and scattered them, some being seriously wounded. ... We were all fagged out with the strenuous work. A shower of rain had rendered the track very greasy and slippery and in many places shells had cut it up. Our patient was severely wounded in the abdomen and had a shell dressing on to keep his bowels in. He seemed in agony and rolled about and we had difficulty in keeping him on the stretcher… It was most difficult to get a footing with the weight of the stretcher. In places the hands and feet of buried men would be protruding out of the walls of the trench and several times we were nearly bogged in the mud.

About: Working as a stretcher bearer.

Agrees with what I know: Being a stretcher bearer was dangerous.

Message: Work as a stretcher bearer was difficult.

Annotate or highlight key points in the sources as you read or look at them. This will help you to find ideas to include in your answer.

Had a look ☐ **Nearly there** ☐ **Nailed it!** ☐

Working with sources

How can I spot a message in a source?

1. Look at the words that have been chosen. Are they positive (like victory or success) or negative (like disaster or failure)?
2. Does the source exaggerate anything? Does it only give examples from one point of view?
3. In illustrations, has the artist made anyone look smart and intelligent, or stupid and ridiculous?

Most sources were not made just to share information. They were designed to share an opinion, to persuade others that something was good or bad, or to make people support something. A historian needs to learn to spot the message.

In Paper 1, you will be asked about sources in Question 2a (which is about the usefulness of a source) and Question 2b (which asks how you would follow up a source). You can find more about these questions on pages 23–30.

Provenance: nature, origin and purpose

The **provenance** of a source is its **nature**, **origin** and **purpose**.

Nature	What type of source is it?	For example, is it a newspaper article, speech, leaflet, letter, diary entry, book, postcard, poster, cartoon or photograph?
Origin	Where is it from?	Who wrote it? Were they involved with the event? Is it from before, after or during the event? Is it from where the events happened or from somewhere else?
Purpose	Why was it made?	Was it made to inform people? Persuade people? Sell something? Give evidence to make a decision? Was it made for the public or for a specific person or group of people?

Identifying the nature, origin and purpose (NOP) of a source is an important skill. It will help you to judge whether a source is likely to be reliable, balanced or accurate. For Paper 1, you will need this skill for Question 2a.

Where can I find the provenance?

Start by looking at the key information about provenance that comes just before the source itself. This can give you a lot of information:

- what the source is
- who made or wrote it
- when they made or wrote it.

Top tip

Always read the key information about provenance first. The source itself may have information about NOP too, but starting with the key information will help you to spot words or details in the source which show the opinion or message of the person who created it.

The source is a photograph.

It was taken during this event, at this place.

Source A: A photograph of stretcher bearers at the Third Battle of Ypres, August 1917, taken by Lieutenant John Brooke, an official British army photographer on the Western Front.

It was taken at this time.

It was taken by an official army photographer.

Had a look ☐ **Nearly there** ☐ **Nailed it!** ☐

Using key terms

Using key terms helps to show you know and understand the topic.

What key terms might I need to use?

anaesthetics – medications that prevent pain by numbing feeling or making people unconscious
antibiotics – medicines that kill bacteria or stop them growing, used to treat bacterial infection
antiseptics – medicines which kill microbes that cause infection
apothecary – a person who mixed medicines to treat illness and injury in the Middle Ages
bleeding/bloodletting – removing blood from a patient to prevent or cure disease
the Church – the Roman Catholic Church, which controlled medieval ideas about medicine
chemotherapy – a type of cancer treatment that stops cancer cells multiplying
cholera – an infectious disease spread through contaminated water, which causes severe diarrhoea
circulation – moving back and forth or around something; blood circulates around the body
diagnosis – the identification of what is wrong when someone is ill
dissection – the act of cutting up a dead body to study it
DNA – deoxyribonucleic acid; the genetic code controlling features like hair and eye colour
epidemic – the rapid spread of an infectious disease to a large number of people
genetics – the study of inherited characteristics and diseases
inoculation – originally the term used for deliberately infecting someone with a disease to prevent a more severe case of it; later used in a similar way to **vaccination**
laissez-faire – the policy of leaving things to take their own course
medieval period/Middle Ages – from the 5th to the 15th century
miasma – 'bad air' produced by rotting matter, which was believed to cause certain diseases
microbe – a living organism that can only be seen with a microscope
modern period – the present day; for this thematic study it means since 1900
observation – the act of closely watching and monitoring something
pandemic – the worldwide spread of an infectious disease
penicillin – the first antibiotic, discovered in 1928
physician – doctor; first used in the Middle Ages
purging – removing food from a person either by making them vomit or by using laxatives
radiotherapy – a treatment which uses radiation to treat disease, especially cancer
Renaissance – literally, 'rebirth'; for this thematic study, it means the period from c1500–c1700
supernatural – something that cannot be explained by science or the laws of nature
vaccination – a process where someone is immunised against a disease (similar to **inoculation**)

Make sure that you can spell scientific or very old words, like **miasma**, correctly.

The key terms shown with capital letters will always use capital letters, wherever they appear in a sentence.

The key terms on this page are the most important ones. If you think of others, write them down in the back of this book.

Top tip

What about dates?

Make sure you can write about dates and time periods accurately. For example:

- The year **1560** was in the **16th century**.
- The **1700s** were the **18th century**.

A century is a period of 100 years. To find the century, knock the last two digits off the year and add one. For example:
1759 ⇨ 17 + 1 = 18 ⇨ 18th century

Remember: 'c' before a year means 'around'. For example, 'c1700' means 'around 1700'.

Had a look ☐ **Nearly there** ☐ **Nailed it!** ☐

SPaG

Good spelling, punctuation and grammar (SPaG) are important in every exam, but in your Paper 1 exam four marks are available specifically for SPaG and your use of specialist terminology.

What are the SPaG marks for?

For Paper 1, SPaG is tested on Question 5/6.

You can get up to four marks for your quality of written communication.

The best responses:

- ✓ have accurate spelling and punctuation throughout the answer
- ✓ use the rules of grammar to write clearly throughout the answer
- ✓ use a wide range of key terms.

What about key terms?

Use key terms to show your topic knowledge, like 'purging' in the stronger example below.

✗ In the Middle Ages, a common treatment was removing food by making the patient sick.

✓ In the Middle Ages, a common treatment was purging.

Tricky words

Some important words are often spelled incorrectly. Make sure you can spell these words:

anaesthetic	apothecary	appearance
beginning	benefited	exaggerate
occurred	physician	purpose
preparation	professional	surgeon

When you find other tricky words, list them at the back of this book.

Formal language

Use...	✓	✗
Standard English, not slang	vaccinations	jabs
Correct grammar	would have	would of

Top tip

Use homophones (words that sound the same but have different meanings) correctly. For example, make sure you know whether to use 'their' or 'there'.

Writing clear sentences

Sentences that are clear start with capital letters, end with full-stops and are not too long.

✗ The Victorians were suspicious of anaesthetics and thought God made things painful on purpose however when Queen Victoria used chloroform during childbirth attitudes started to change.

✓ The Victorians were suspicious of anaesthetics. They thought God made things painful on purpose. However, when Queen Victoria used chloroform during childbirth, attitudes started to change.

The second example, with shorter sentences, is easier to read.

Punctuation for meaning

Use punctuation to make your meaning clear:

- Use commas to separate ideas or information.
- Use commas between items in a list.
- Use apostrophes to show that something belongs to something else.

The apostrophe shows that the urine belongs to the patient.

✓ Physicians examined a patient's urine to help diagnose their illness. They would smell, taste and check the colour of the urine.

The comma separates the first two items in the list.

Had a look ☐ **Nearly there** ☐ **Nailed it!** ☐

Understanding your exam

It is a good idea to understand how your exam paper works. You will know what to expect and this will help you to feel confident when you are in the exam.

Paper 1 thematic study and historic environment

Your thematic study is your Paper 1 exam. Paper 1 is...

- a written exam
- 1 hour 15 minutes
- worth 52 marks
- worth 30% of your GCSE History.

What will I get in the exam?

- You will get an exam paper. The paper has spaces to write your answers in.
- You will also get a Sources Booklet. This will contain two sources which you will need to use to answer the questions in Section A of the exam paper.

Section A is on the historic environment and Section B is on the thematic study.

What is a thematic study and what is a historic environment?

This paper – Medicine in Britain, c1250–present – explores a long period of British history, nearly 800 years in length. It is called a thematic study because instead of focusing on one specific period, you will look at themes through the period, exploring what changes and what stays the same. As part of the topic, you will study a historic environment – a case study of a location during a specific period of time. In this case, the historic environment is the British sector of the Western Front, 1914–18: injuries, treatment and the trenches.

What historical skills does Paper 1 assess?

Your GCSE History exam papers are designed to assess different historical skills, or 'Assessment Objectives' (AOs).

Your Paper 1 thematic study and historic environment will assess these assessment objectives:

AO1 – Demonstrate knowledge and understanding of the key features of the period.

This means you need to show your knowledge of the topic, including details of the main events, people and themes.

AO2 – Explain and analyse events using second-order historical concepts.

This means you need to analyse historical ideas in your answers – these ideas are called **second-order historical concepts**.

The second-order historical concepts are: causation (why things happened), consequences (the results of something), similarity, difference, change, continuity (staying the same) and significance (how important an event, idea or change was).

AO3 – Analyse, evaluate and use sources to make substantiated judgements.

This means you need to use historical sources to investigate a topic, and make judgements about how useful they are.

You can find out more about working with sources on pages 13–14.

Substantiated means backing something up. A substantiated judgement is a judgement which is supported with a reason.

Had a look ☐ Nearly there ☐ Nailed it! ☐

Understanding your exam

What type of questions will be on the exam for Paper 1?

The questions for Paper 1 will always follow the same pattern:

SECTION A: historic environment

1 Describe **two** features of…

(4 marks)

Question 1 is the **describing** question:

- (4) Worth 4 marks
- Tests AO1
- Spend about 5 minutes
- ✓ Describe **two** different features of the topic.

2a Study Sources A and B.

How useful are Sources A and B for an enquiry into…?

(8 marks)

Question 2a is the **assessing usefulness** question:

- (8) Worth 8 marks
- Tests AO3
- Spend about 14 minutes
- ✓ Use both sources and your own knowledge.

2b Study Source A/B.

How could you follow up Source A/B to find out more about…?

(4 marks)

Question 2b is the **follow-up enquiry** question:

- (4) Worth 4 marks
- Tests AO3
- Spend about 5 minutes
- ✓ Show how you would continue an enquiry.

SECTION B: thematic study

3 Explain **one** way in which… was/were similar/different…

(4 marks)

Question 3 is the **making comparisons** question:

- (4) Worth 4 marks
- Tests AO1 and AO2
- Spend about 5 minutes
- ✓ Explain **one** similarity or difference.

4 Explain why…

(12 marks)

Question 4 is the **explaining why** question:

- (12) Worth 12 marks
- Tests AO1 and AO2
- Spend about 18 minutes
- ✓ You must use some of your own information.

5/6 'A statement.'

How far do you agree?

(16 marks plus 4 marks for SPaG and use of specialist terminology)

Question 5/6 is the **judgement** question:

- (16) + (4) Worth 16 marks, plus 4 for SPaG
- Tests AO1 and AO2
- Spend about 25 minutes
- ✓ You need to reach a judgement.

Had a look ☐ **Nearly there** ☐ **Nailed it!** ☐

Understanding Question 1

Question 1 will always be structured in the same way. Make sure you know how this question works and what it is asking you to do.

How does Question 1 work?

Identify the command word – this question will always ask you to 'describe'.

This tells you that you need to write about **two** separate features.

> 1 Describe **two** features of the treatment of infections on the Western Front during the First World War.
>
> **(4 marks)**

Check how many marks the question is worth – this will help you to manage your time.

This is the topic for the question. The two features you describe must be linked to this topic.

Links This question is similar to Question 1a on Paper 2 (your British depth study).

What does Question 1 assess?

- ✓ Question 1 tests Assessment Objective 1.
- ✓ You need to show your knowledge of the topic.
- ✓ This will involve giving details of features related to the historic environment – the British sector of the Western Front, 1914–18.

How long should I spend?

Spend about 5 minutes on Question 1.

Try not to spend longer than this as the next questions will need plenty of time.

Take a look at page 17 for more about the assessment objectives.

What does 'describe' mean?

Describe means that your answer should show that you understand what the topic in the question is. You don't need to give reasons for it, or say how important it was. You just need to give two separate pieces of information about the topic.

Top tip The key thing to remember is that you can pick any two features but they **must** be connected to the topic in the question.

What is a 'feature'?

A **feature** is a relevant piece of information about the topic. This could be what happened, who was involved, how it affected people or any other detail about the topic. For example, with the question above about the treatment of infections, you could mention:

- surgical methods of treating infection
- chemical methods of treating infection
- any other relevant features.

Had a look ☐ Nearly there ☐ Nailed it! ☐

Understanding Question 1

Features and supporting information

Each feature you describe in your answer needs supporting information. This means you need to add a bit more detail to each feature you identify. For example, for the question on infections on page 19, you could have this feature and supporting information:

> One feature was removing the infected tissue by cutting it away.

This is a **valid feature** of the treatment of infections on the Western Front. This would get one mark.

> This was done as soon as possible to try to stop the infection spreading.

This is **supporting information** that adds to the feature about removing infected tissue. It is not a new feature. This would get one mark.

How is Question 1 marked?

Marks are available for identifying the features and for providing supporting information.

- There is **one mark available for each valid feature** you identify – so one mark for giving one feature, and two marks for giving two features. Adding more features does not improve your mark.
- There is **one mark available** for adding supporting information to one of your features, and **two marks** if you add supporting information to both of your features.

Using language to write clear answers

To make your answer clear, you could introduce each feature like this:

> One feature was...
>
> A second feature was...

Top tip

Remember to use **key terms** in your answer.

Turn to page 12 for more about writing clear answers. You can find examples of key terms on page 15.

Top tips for success

Top tip

- ✓ Describe **two different features** – take care not to use the same feature twice.
- ✓ Use **valid** features – make sure that both features are connected to the topic in the question.
- ✓ For each feature, write two sentences – one to **identify** the feature and one to add **supporting information** that is connected to that feature.
- ✓ Keep your answers **concise** – don't write more than you need to.
- ✓ **Use the space** on the exam paper – there will be a space marked for each feature.
- ✓ Be specific – avoid very general, vague sentences, like 'people got infections when they were wounded'.
- ✓ Be accurate – use correct facts to support your features.

Had a look ☐ Nearly there ☐ Nailed it! ☐

Answering Question 1

You need to understand how you can write a successful answer to Question 1.

Reading the question

1 Describe **two** features of the treatment of infections on the Western Front during the First World War.

(4 marks)

Always read the question carefully before you start writing your answer. Make sure you are clear about what the topic of the question is.

Short, 4-mark questions do not need a plan.

Steps to success

1 Identify **one** valid feature of the topic. Write **one** sentence about it.

Feature 1

One feature was that antiseptic and aseptic conditions were not possible in dressing stations and casualty clearing stations.

Answer in the correct space on the page. Describe your first feature in the space for 'Feature 1'.

Identify one valid feature which is relevant to the topic.

2 **Add information** to support your first feature, using your knowledge of the topic. Write **one** sentence.

Chemicals were used during surgery to try to kill the bacteria causing the infection instead.

Add a sentence of supporting information.

Make sure the supporting information is connected to your first feature. It should not be an unconnected fact.

3 Identify a **second** valid feature of the topic. Write **one** sentence about it.

Feature 2

A second feature was that surgeons tried to remove infected tissue when taking out a bullet or shrapnel.

Identify a second feature which is relevant to the topic.

Make sure your second feature is different to your first feature.

4 **Add information** to support your first feature, using your knowledge of the topic. Write **one** sentence.

Surgeons developed techniques to do this because infections were often very deep in the body and other methods such as using chemicals did not always work.

Add a sentence of supporting information.

Make sure the supporting information is connected to your second feature.

Had a look ☐ **Nearly there** ☐ **Nailed it!** ☐

Answering Question 1

Getting it right

Question 1 should be a good chance to get some straightforward marks at the beginning of your exam paper. Stay focused on the question and don't write more than you need to. Look at these examples.

Feature 1

One feature was that only a limited number of infections were treated successfully on the Western Front. **(1)** Many soldiers were treated in dressing stations and casualty clearing stations where it was difficult to maintain antiseptic and aseptic conditions. **(1)**

Feature 2

Poor hygiene on the Western Front often made treating infection difficult.

✓ This gives one valid feature – that not many infections were treated successfully – which would get 1 mark. The supporting information – which gives more information about why treatment was often unsuccessful – would also get 1 mark.

✗ The second feature repeats the first feature, so does not get any marks. To improve, this answer needs a second feature that is different to the first.

Feature 1

One feature was that methods for treating infected wounds changed throughout the war. **(1)** Most injuries were caused by shrapnel from explosive shells.

Feature 2

A second feature was that the Carrel-Dakin method had been developed by 1917 and was an effective way of treating many infections. **(1)** Blood transfusions also helped the wounded survive.

✓ This is a valid feature.

✗ This supporting information is not connected to the feature so does not get any marks. The supporting information should be about the changing methods used to treat infected wounds.

✗ This is also a valid feature, but again the supporting information is not connected to the feature so does not get a mark. It should be about the Carrel-Dakin method. Blood transfusions did not directly help treat infections.

Feature 1

One feature was that infected limbs often had to be amputated to remove the infection and prevent it spreading. **(1)** Later, as surgery developed, it was possible to remove just the infected tissue. **(1)**

Feature 2

A second feature was that by 1917 the Carrel-Dakin method had been developed and was an effective treatment for many infections. **(1)** This method involved pouring sterilised salt solution through the wound using tubes. **(1)**

✓ This is a valid feature. It also has supporting information that develops the feature. Feature 1 would get 2 marks.

✓ This is a second, different feature, which also has supporting information. So Feature 2 would get 2 marks.

Did you notice that the features in this strong answer are different from the ones in the answer on page 21? It doesn't matter which features you describe as long as they are accurate and valid.

Had a look ☐ **Nearly there** ☐ **Nailed it!** ☐

Understanding Question 2a

Question 2a will always be structured in the same way. Make sure you know how this question works and what it is asking you to do.

How does Question 2a work?

In the exam, Sources A and B will be in a Source Booklet. For this question, you will find Sources A and B on page 13.

Identify the command word – this question will always ask you to consider 'how useful' the sources are for a particular enquiry.

> **2a** Study Sources A and B on page 13.
>
> How useful are Sources A and B for an enquiry into the problems involved in transporting the wounded to medical treatment on the Western Front?
>
> Explain your answer, using Sources A and B and your knowledge of the historical context.
>
> **(8 marks)**

This is the **enquiry** (area of investigation) you need to focus on.

Check how many marks the question is worth – this will help you to manage your time.

You must refer to both sources and use your own knowledge.

Links This question is similar to Question 3a on Paper 3 (your modern depth study).

What does Question 2a assess?

- Question 2a tests Assessment Objective 3.
- You need to use historical sources to investigate a topic.
- You need to make judgements about how useful the sources are for the enquiry given in the question.

How long should I spend?

Spend about 14 minutes on Question 2a.

Remember that you need to look at **both** sources. Divide your time equally between them so you give them equal attention in your answer.

Take a look at page 17 for more about the assessment objectives.

Why do I need to focus on the enquiry in the question?

Top tip

Imagine a toolbox. It has different tools, such as hammers, screwdrivers and saws. Each tool is useful in one way or another. But **how** useful each tool is depends on the job you need to do. For example, if you need to hit a nail into a wall, a hammer is useful, whereas a saw is not – but if you need to cut a piece of wood, the saw is a very useful tool.

All sources are useful in some way. But, depending on the enquiry topic, their usefulness will change. For example, look at Source B on page 13. It is very useful for investigating some enquiries, like the difficulties faced by stretcher bearers, but less useful for studying the medical treatment the wounded received. So, **when you consider how useful the sources are for Question 2a, make sure you stay focused on the enquiry in the question.**

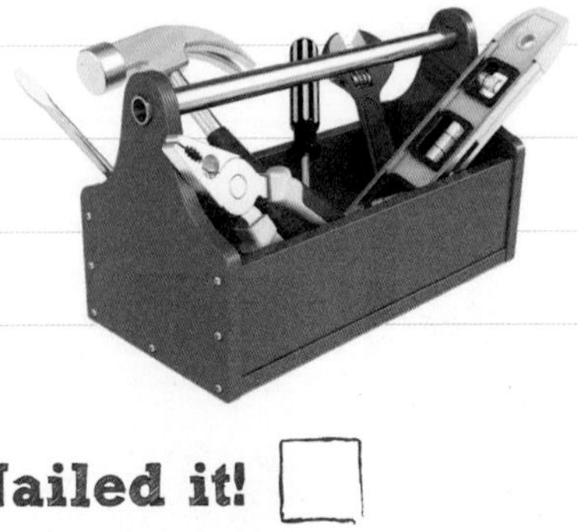

Had a look ☐ **Nearly there** ☐ **Nailed it!** ☐

Understanding Question 2a

How to judge usefulness

To judge **usefulness** you need to assess how useful the source is for the enquiry in the question.

To measure usefulness you need to think about two things:

- How much you can learn about the enquiry topic from the content of the source.
- If the source is giving you accurate information.

What's in the source?

Pick out points from the content of the source which give information about the enquiry topic. If the source contains information that is relevant then it is useful for the enquiry.

Compare the content to your own knowledge. If the source supports what you know about the topic, it is more useful.

Remember: Focus on what **is** in the source, not on what is missing. Missing content is only important if it should be in the source but isn't.

Is the information accurate?

You need to consider whether the information in the source is accurate:

- Is it balanced? For example, a balanced, confidential account written for a government department making policies might be likely to contain accurate details.
- Or is it presenting the information in a one-sided or exaggerated way? For example, a newspaper cartoon which is criticising a politician might be exaggerated.

Generally, a source which is more accurate and more balanced will be more useful than one that is exaggerated and one-sided. However, if the enquiry is about people's opinions, sometimes a one-sided, exaggerated source is more useful for showing what people thought.

Look at the **provenance** – **nature, origin and purpose** – of the source. Does this make the source more or less useful?

You can find more about nature, origin and purpose on page 14.

Remember: A source can be useful even if it is unreliable. For example, personal accounts such as Source B on page 13 will always be one-sided as they are just one person's point of view. Also, a person's memories of events may not be accurate. However, sources like this are still useful in enquiries about people's experiences or opinions as they show what people thought at the time.

How is Question 2a marked?

Strong answers to Question 2a:

- ✓ judge the usefulness of each source for the enquiry given in the question
- ✓ explain clearly how the provenance of each source makes it more or less useful
- ✓ support judgements with comments on each source's content and provenance
- ✓ use own knowledge to interpret the sources and support their judgements.

You don't need to compare the sources and you don't need to decide which one is more useful. Write about one source, then the other – without comparing them.

Top tips for success

Top tip

- ✓ Stay focused on the enquiry given in the question – **decide how useful each source is for this enquiry.**
- ✓ Refer to **both sources** – judge the usefulness of each one.
- ✓ Analyse the **content** and **provenance** of **each source** – **explain why** this makes the source more or less useful.
- ✓ Use **your own knowledge of the topic** to judge the source – does it agree with what you know?
- ✓ Make a **quick plan** before you write to help you to stay focused.

Had a look ☐ Nearly there ☐ Nailed it! ☐

Answering Question 2a

You need to understand how you can write a successful answer to Question 2a.

Reading the question

2a Study Sources A and B on page 13.

How useful are Sources A and B for an enquiry into the problems involved in transporting the wounded to medical treatment on the Western Front?

Explain your answer, using Sources A and B and your knowledge of the historical context.

(8 marks)

Always read the question carefully before you start writing your answer.

Make sure you are clear about what the enquiry topic of the question is.

Top tip

Remember: No source in the exam will ever be useless for the enquiry. You can say it is not very useful but don't say it is useless.

Writing about usefulness

Use phrases such as 'quite useful', 'very useful' and 'partially useful' to give a clear judgement about the usefulness of a source.

How can I structure my answer?

1. Explain how useful the content of **Source A** is for the enquiry. Use at least one example from the source.
2. Explain how the provenance affects the usefulness of **Source A**. Finish with an overall judgement about usefulness.
3. Repeat Steps 1 and 2 for **Source B**.

Top tip

Remember that you don't need to compare the sources.

You can find more about nature, origin and purpose on page 14.

Plan your answer

This question is worth 8 marks, so note down a quick plan before you start writing.

The best answers are well organised. Structure your plan clearly to keep your answer focused.

Keep it short. You don't need full sentences.

Source A	Source B
• Shows v. muddy terrain • Know that weather v. bad at 3rd Battle Ypres • Photo: genuine though could be staged • V. useful	• Describes bad terrain and impact on SBs + patient • Know about poor conditions + danger to SBs • Diary: truthful but one-sided • V. useful

Include your own knowledge.

Combine NOP notes in one point.

Include a judgement about each source.

This is one style of plan. You can see another style on page 37.

Had a look ☐ **Nearly there** ☐ **Nailed it!** ☐

Answering Question 2a

Steps to success

1 Explain how useful the content of **Source A** is for the enquiry topic in the question.

Start with a quick judgement about the source. This will help you to focus on usefulness.

Source A is very useful for an enquiry into the problems involved in transporting the wounded to medical treatment on the Western Front. It is useful because it shows a very large, muddy area and seven stretcher bearers struggling to cross it carrying just one wounded man, which highlights how the boggy terrain made transportation difficult. The source suggests that it would have taken a long time to get the wounded to medical treatment so injuries and infections were likely to get worse. It supports what I know about the Third Battle of Ypres which is that it took place in very poor conditions due to heavy rain which led to waterlogging of the ground.

Explain how your points are linked to the enquiry topic. Use the word 'because' to show you are explaining.

Pick out points from the content of the source that are directly relevant to the enquiry. If the source is an image, like this one, identify relevant parts of the image.

Use key terms to show your knowledge of the topic.

Use your own knowledge about the topic to explain how the content of the source fits with the enquiry topic.

Focus on a few key points only – you won't have time to cover every detail.

2 Go on to explain how the provenance affects the usefulness of **Source A** for the enquiry topic in the question.

Source A is a photograph taken by an official British army photographer so it is probably an accurate depiction of conditions. However the photograph could have been staged to some extent. For example, the photographer could have chosen a particularly muddy spot to take the photograph or asked more stretcher bearers to be in the image to emphasise the difficulties. However, it would have been impossible to completely stage the image in war conditions so we can assume it is generally accurate, which makes it more useful. Therefore, I think Source A is very useful because it powerfully shows the reality of the terrain and how it made getting the wounded to medical treatment very difficult.

Use NOP to help you decide whether the source is balanced or one-sided – this answer uses the nature of the source.

Explain whether the source is balanced and accurate (or not) and why. Remember: balanced, accurate sources are more reliable.

Explain how the source's reliability affects its usefulness.

Finish your analysis of Source A with an overall judgement about its usefulness.

Give a clear reason for your judgement and link it back to the enquiry topic.

3 Repeat Steps 1 and 2 for **Source B**. Explain how useful the content of **Source B** is for the enquiry topic, then explain how the provenance affects its usefulness for the enquiry topic. Remember to finish with an overall judgement about **Source B**'s usefulness.

Had a look ☐ **Nearly there** ☐ **Nailed it!** ☐

Understanding Question 2b

Question 2b will always be structured in the same way. Make sure you know how this question works and what it is asking you to do.

How does Question 2b work?

Identify the source you need to focus on – this question will ask about **either** Source A **or** Source B.

This is the **enquiry** you need to focus on. The enquiry will always be the same as the enquiry in Question 2a.

This question gives you a table to complete – you should use this to structure your answer.

This question will always ask **how** you could **follow up** the source.

Check how many marks the question is worth – this will help you to manage your time.

> **2b** Study Source B on page 13.
>
> How could you follow up Source B to find out more about the problems involved in transporting the wounded to medical treatment on the Western Front?
>
> In your answer, you must give the question you would ask and the type of source you could use.
>
> Complete the table below.
>
> **(4 marks)**

What does Question 2b assess?

- Question 2b tests Assessment Objective 3.
- You need to show you can design questions to carry out a historical enquiry.
- You need to show that you understand the types of source that a historian might use to investigate a historical enquiry.

How long should I spend?

Spend about 5 minutes on Question 2b.

Try not to spend longer than this as the next questions will need plenty of time.

Take a look at page 17 for more about the assessment objectives.

What does 'follow up' mean?

Follow up means that you need to design a question which a historian could use to find out more about something they have learned from the source. This includes identifying where they could go to find the answer.

Top tip

You must stay focused on the enquiry in the question. This is especially important when you design your follow-up question.

What are the parts of the answer?

1. Identify a **detail** in the source to follow up.
2. Give a **follow-up question** you would ask about the detail you have identified.
3. Suggest a **type of source** you could use to answer your follow-up question.
4. Explain **how** this type of source would help you to answer your follow-up question.

Had a look ☐ Nearly there ☐ Nailed it! ☐

Understanding Question 2b

Identifying a detail in the source

You can pick any detail from the source, but:

- the detail **must** be relevant to the enquiry
- you must identify a **specific** detail
- the detail must be **from the source itself**, and not from the information about provenance.

Top tip

Make sure you give a detail rather than writing a question for this part of the answer. Quoting a phrase from the source is a good way to do this if the source is a text.

Forming a question

Your follow-up question **must** be:

- linked to the enquiry in the question
- linked to the detail you have already identified in the source.

Your question should be one you could find the answer to, and that would help you to understand the enquiry better. For example, you could ask about:

- the reason for the detail
- the consequence of the detail
- whether the detail happened a lot.

Suggesting a type of source

The type of source you choose must help to answer your follow-up question and must be **specific**. These are examples of specific sources:

✓ articles in medical journals detailing treatments given by medical workers on the Western Front

✓ records of injuries/treatments from Casualty Clearing Stations

✓ personal accounts from soldiers detailing medical treatment received.

Avoid vague general sources like these:

✗ medical records

✗ soldiers' diaries.

Explaining how the source will help

You need to explain how the type of source you have identified could help to answer your follow-up question. What sort of information would the source contain? How could you use this?

Keep your explanation precise. For example:

✓ I would be able to see how many people were treated for this type of injury.

Avoid general explanations, like this:

✗ It would tell me what I want to know.

How is Question 2b marked?

There is **one mark available for each part of the question**. This means:

✓ one mark for identifying a valid detail in the source

✓ one mark for a follow-up question linked to the detail chosen

✓ one mark for a type of source that could be used to answer the follow-up question

✓ one mark for an explanation of how the source could help to answer the follow-up question.

You must make sure the parts of your answer link together.

Top tips for success

Top tip

✓ Stay focused on the enquiry.

✓ Identify **one specific detail** from the content of the source.

✓ Give a follow-up question that is linked to the detail you have chosen **and** to the enquiry in the question.

✓ Choose a **specific** type of source to help answer your follow-up question.

✓ Explain **precisely** how the type of source will help answer the follow-up question.

✓ Keep all parts of your answer **concise**.

✓ **Use the table** on the exam paper.

Had a look ☐ **Nearly there** ☐ **Nailed it!** ☐

Answering Question 2b

You need to understand how you can write a successful answer to Question 2b.

Reading the question

2b Study Source B on page 13.

How could you follow up Source B to find out more about the problems involved in transporting the wounded to medical treatment on the Western Front?

In your answer, you must give the question you would ask and the type of source you could use.

Complete the table below.

(4 marks)

Always read the question carefully before you start writing your answer.

Always check which source the question is about.

Short, 4-mark questions do not need a plan.

Steps to success

1 Identify **one** valid detail in Source B.

Detail in Source B that I would follow up:

'Several times we were nearly bogged in the mud.'

Choose a specific and relevant detail from the source itself.

If the source is a text, quote a phrase from it.

2 Write down a follow-up question that would help you to understand the enquiry better.

Question I would ask:

Was mud and boggy terrain a problem in retrieving the wounded in many battles?

Make sure your question relates to the detail you have identified.

Make sure your question is also linked to the enquiry.

3 Identify a type of source that you could use to find an answer to your follow-up question.

What type of source I could use:

Field ambulance reports from different battles on the Western Front.

Give one type of source.

Choose a specific type of source. Here, just writing 'Field ambulance records' would be too general.

4 Explain how your source could help you to answer your follow-up question.

How this might help answer my question:

These reports would give the conditions in each battle and the impact this had on retrieving the wounded.

Make sure your explanation is related to the enquiry and the type of source you have chosen.

Make sure that you keep your explanation precise.

Had a look ☐ **Nearly there** ☐ **Nailed it!** ☐

Answering Question 2b

Getting it right

Question 2b should be a good chance to get some straightforward marks. Stay focused on the question and don't write more than you need to. Look at these examples.

Detail in Source B that I would follow up:
'a shell burst nearby and scattered them, some being seriously wounded' **(1)**

Question I would ask:
How often did those transporting the wounded come under attack? **(1)**

What type of source I could use:
Army records

How this might help answer my question:
These would tell me the types of injuries people got.

✓ The detail given is valid – it is specific, from the source itself, and it could be connected to the problems involved in transporting the wounded to medical treatment.

✓ The follow-up question is connected to the detail given above and to the enquiry of problems involved in transporting the wounded.

✗ This type of source is too vague – it needs to be more specific. It is also not related to the follow-up question given above.

✗ This is too vague and doesn't give enough explanation. It is also not related to the follow-up question given above.

Detail in Source B that I would follow up:
'Our patient was severely wounded in the abdomen and had a shell dressing on.' **(1)**

Question I would ask:
What treatments did stretcher bearers carry out on the front line?

What type of source I could use:
Training manuals for stretcher bearers describing and explaining treatments to be given.

How this might help answer my question:
The training manuals would give details of what stretcher bearers should do when presented with different injuries which would include treatments.

✓ This detail is valid.

✗ This is not a valid question because, although it's connected to the detail, it isn't related to the enquiry – problems involved in transporting the wounded to medical treatment.

✗ This gives a specific source, but it's linked to the follow-up question, which isn't related to the enquiry, so this wouldn't gain a mark.

✗ This explanation is precise, but it's linked to the follow-up question, which isn't related to the enquiry, so it wouldn't get a mark.

Compare the examples above with the strong answer on page 29. To write a successful answer in the exam:

- stay focused on the enquiry given in the question throughout your answer
- make sure the parts of your answer link together.

Had a look ☐ **Nearly there** ☐ **Nailed it!** ☐

Understanding Question 3

Question 3 will always be structured in the same way. Make sure you know how this question works and what it is asking you to do.

How does Question 3 work?

This tells you that you need to write about just **one** difference. This question will always ask **either** about a difference **or** a similarity.

These are the two time periods that you need to compare – the question will always give you two separate periods.

Identify the command word – this question will always ask you to 'explain'.

> 3 Explain **one** way in which explanations of the causes of disease were different in the seventeenth and nineteenth centuries.
>
> (4 marks)

Check how many marks the question is worth – this will help you to manage your time.

This is the topic for the question.

You will always need to make a comparison between two time periods – either how something was similar in the two periods, or how it was different.

What does Question 3 assess?

- ✓ Question 3 tests Assessment Objectives 1 and 2.
- ✓ You need to show your knowledge of the topic.
- ✓ You also need to show you can explain and analyse similarity or difference between two periods of time.

How long should I spend?

Spend about 5 minutes on Question 3.

Try not to spend longer than this as the next questions will need plenty of time.

Take a look at page 17 for more about the assessment objectives.

What does 'explain' mean?

For Question 3, you need to make a comparison – you need to **explain** one way in which something was similar or different over time. To do this, you need to:

- **identify a difference or a similarity** (whichever the question asks for)
- **give specific examples from each time period** to support the difference or similarity you have identified.

Remember!

Top tip

- You only need to explain **one** similarity/difference.
- You need to explain **how** it was different – not why.
- You need to make sure you understand time periods and the different ways they can be written – to make sure you give examples from the right period.

You can find out more about dates on page 15.

Had a look ☐ Nearly there ☐ Nailed it! ☐

Understanding Question 3

Identifying a difference/similarity

- Make sure you are clear about the topic in the question.
- Identify a difference/similarity that is **linked to the topic** in the question.
- State the difference/similarity you identify **clearly** in your answer – it is best to do this before you go on to give evidence from each time period.

If you are asked about a similarity, you need to identify something that did not change between the time periods. If you are asked about a difference, you need to identify something that did change.

Supporting your comparison

- Give **examples from each time period** to explain the difference/similarity you have identified.
- Make sure the examples are **relevant** to the difference/similarity you have identified.
- Make sure your examples from each time period **link up** with each other – otherwise you are not showing a difference/similarity.

Top tip

Keep your supporting information **balanced** and **specific**:

✓ Give examples from **each** time period.

✗ Don't just say it was different/the same in the other time period.

How is Question 3 marked?

Strong answers to Question 3:

✓ analyse features of the period to explain a difference or similarity

✓ give specific information about the topic to support the comparison

✓ show good knowledge and understanding of both time periods.

Top tip

Remember to use **key terms** in your answer.

Turn to page 12 for more about writing clear answers.
You can find examples of key terms on page 15.

Using language to write clear answers

To make your answer clear, you could introduce the similarity or difference like this:

One way in which [the topic] was different/similar was…

You could introduce your examples like this:

In [the first period]…

In comparison, during [the second period]…

Top tips for success

Top tip

✓ State one difference/similarity **clearly** at the beginning of your answer.

✓ Make sure your difference/similarity is **linked to the topic** in the question.

✓ Give **examples from each time period** to support your difference/similarity and keep your answer balanced.

✓ Make sure your examples are **relevant** and **specific**, and that they are linked.

✓ Use **key terms** to show your knowledge and understanding.

✓ Keep your answers **concise** – don't write more than you need to.

✓ Be **specific** – avoid general comparisons (like 'later they were different').

✓ Be **accurate** – use correct facts to support your comparison.

Had a look ☐ **Nearly there** ☐ **Nailed it!** ☐

Answering Question 3

You need to understand how you can write a successful answer to Question 3.

Reading the question

> 3 Explain **one** way in which explanations of the causes of disease were different in the seventeenth and nineteenth centuries.
>
> (4 marks)

Always read the question carefully before you start writing your answer. Make sure you are clear about what the topic of the question is.

Check carefully whether you need to write about a similarity or a difference.

Identify which two time periods you are being asked to compare.

Short, 4-mark questions do not need a plan.

Steps to success

1 Identify **one** difference/similarity – depending on what the question asks for.

> One way in which explanations of the causes of disease were different was that in the seventeenth century many people still believed God caused disease but by the nineteenth century most people had started to accept scientific ideas.

Use clear language to focus your answer.

Start by clearly stating the difference or similarity between the two periods.

2 Focus on the earlier time period. Give an example of what happened in this period.

> In the 1660s, for example, many people believed that the outbreak of plague was caused by God being angry with people. They prayed to God to spare them from the plague or cure them if they caught it.

Make sure your example is relevant to the difference or similarity you have identified.

Keep your example specific and concise.

3 Focus on the later time period. Give an example of how this was similar/different to the earlier time period.

> In comparison, by the nineteenth century, far fewer people still believed that God caused disease and most people believed there was a rational or scientific explanation for disease. For example, the number of people vaccinated against smallpox increased from 1800 as more and more people accepted that this scientific method prevented this disease.

Use clear language to show that you are comparing the two periods. You could also use, for example, 'however' or 'this changed when...'

Use key terms to show your knowledge of the topic.

Make sure your example is relevant to your difference/similarity.

Had a look ☐ **Nearly there** ☐ **Nailed it!** ☐

Answering Question 3

Getting it right

Question 3 should be a good chance to get some straightforward marks. Stay focused on the question and don't write more than you need to. Look at these examples.

One way in which explanations of the causes of disease were different in these periods was that in the nineteenth century scientific explanations were more popular than rational ones. In the seventeenth century, because the Church had less influence, fewer people believed that God made them ill to test them. In the nineteenth century, even fewer people thought God caused disease but some still believed in rational explanations.

✓ A difference is clearly identified at the start of the answer.

✗ These examples do not support the difference identified in the opening sentence.

In the seventeenth century, most people still believed in rational explanations. They believed in the theory of miasma, which said that disease was transmitted by 'bad air', instead of science, whereas in the nineteenth century it was different.

✗ No clear statement of difference is given at the start of the answer.

✓ This is a relevant, specific example from the earlier time period.

✗ This reference to the later time period isn't detailed or specific enough, which makes the explanation unbalanced.

One way in which explanations of the causes of disease were different in these periods was that in the nineteenth century scientific explanations were more popular than rational ones. In the seventeenth century, some people believed in rational explanations. Miasma, which said that disease was transmitted by 'bad air', was a popular theory during epidemics like the Great Plague in 1665. However, in the nineteenth century many people began to believe scientific ideas, and by 1900 most people accepted Pasteur's Germ Theory, which said that microbes caused decay, and the work of Koch, who proved that microbes also caused disease.

✓ The opening sentence clearly states a difference between the two time periods.

✓ This is a specific example from the earlier time period which is also relevant to the difference identified in the opening statement.

✓ This is a specific example from the later time period which is also relevant to the difference identified in the opening statement.

Had a look ☐ Nearly there ☐ Nailed it! ☐

Understanding Question 4

Question 4 will always be structured in the same way. Make sure you know how this question works and what it is asking you to do.

How does Question 4 work?

Identify the command phrase – this question will always ask you to 'explain why'.

This is the change that you need to explain.

4 Explain why the treatment of disease changed very slowly in the years c1500–c1700.

(12 marks)

You may use the following in your answer:

- Andreas Vesalius
- the miasma theory

You **must** also use information of your own.

The question will always have dates, so make sure that you write about the correct time period.

Check how many marks the question is worth – this will help you to manage your time.

Look at the two suggestions – they might be helpful in deciding what to write about.

You **must** include at least one reason from your own knowledge.

Links This question is similar to Question 1b on Paper 2 (your British depth study) and Question 2 on Paper 3 (your modern depth study).

What does Question 4 assess?

- Question 4 tests Assessment Objectives 1 and 2.
- You need to show your knowledge of the topic.
- You need to explain and analyse what caused change.

Take a look at page 17 for more about the assessment objectives.

How long should I spend?

Spend about 18 minutes on Question 4.

This question is worth 12 marks so leave yourself enough time to do a good job. But don't spend too long – you will need to leave enough time for the 16-mark essay question.

What does 'explain why' mean?

Explaining why means giving reasons for something. It is different to just describing a topic. For example, if you were asked 'what was school like today?' you would describe your day. But if you were asked 'why did you go to school today?' you would give reasons why you went to school. It is the same with this question – you need to write an analysis, giving three reasons that explain the change in the question.

What will Question 4 focus on?

Question 4 could ask you about any aspect of Medicine in Britain you have studied. It will cover a broad topic, such as the prevention of disease, over a large time-scale. The question will ask you to explain the reasons why something changed or why it stayed the same.

Top tip The key thing to remember is that you need three reasons and each one needs to be connected to the question topic.

Had a look ☐ **Nearly there** ☐ **Nailed it!** ☐

Understanding Question 4

Choosing reasons

Question 4 will always include two bullet points. **These bullet points are only suggestions – you don't have to use them.** This type of question will always have several possible reasons. So if you don't know what one of the bullet points means, or you don't feel confident writing a paragraph about it, you can replace it with a reason of your own.

For example, the question on page 35 suggests 'Andreas Vesalius' and 'the miasma theory'. If you were answering this question, you could write about these reasons. However, you need **three** reasons in your answer, so you would need to add at least one idea of your own – for example, the poor quality of medical instruments.

Remember: Even if you replace one or both bullet points with another reason, you still need to give **three reasons** overall. At least one of the reasons needs to be your own information.

How is Question 4 marked?

Strong answers to Question 4:

- ✓ give an analytical explanation which is tightly focused on the question throughout
- ✓ keep the explanation clear and well organised throughout
- ✓ include information that is accurate, relevant and closely linked to the question
- ✓ show a wide range of knowledge and understanding of the topic.

Using language to write clear answers

To make your answer clear, you could start each paragraph like this:

One reason was…

A second reason was…

A third reason was…

Turn to page 12 for more about writing clear answers.

Writing analytically

You need to make sure you are **explaining why**. This is called 'writing analytically'. Use phrases like these to show how each reason led to the change in the question:

- This led to…
- As a result…
- Consequently…
- This increased/reduced…
- This showed that…

Top tip

Remember to use **key terms** in your answer.

You can find examples of key terms on page 15.

You don't need to write an introduction or a conclusion for Question 4.

Top tips for success

Top tip

- ✓ Give **three reasons** in your explanation.
- ✓ Include **information of your own.**
- ✓ **Plan** your answer before you write – this will help you to stay focused on the question throughout your answer.
- ✓ Structure your answer clearly using **PEEL paragraphs.**
- ✓ **Explain clearly** why each reason caused the change in the question.
- ✓ Support each reason with **clear and accurate information** about the topic.
- ✓ Make sure you stick to the date range given in the question – only include information from that period.

Had a look ☐ **Nearly there** ☐ **Nailed it!** ☐

Answering Question 4

You need to understand how you can write a successful answer to Question 4.

Reading the question

4 Explain why the treatment of disease changed very slowly in the years c1500–c1700.

(12 marks)

You may use the following in your answer:

- Andreas Vesalius
- the miasma theory

You **must** also use information of your own.

Always read the question carefully before you start writing your answer. Make sure you are clear on the topic.

Check the number of marks. This will help you to use your time well in the exam.

How can I structure my answer?

1. Write about your first reason in one PEEL paragraph.
2. Write about your second reason in one PEEL paragraph.
3. Write about your third reason in one PEEL paragraph.

Remember **PEEL: Point – Evidence – Explain – Link.**

You can find out more about paragraphing and the PEEL structure on page 12.

Plan your answer

This question is worth 12 marks, so take a minute or two to make a quick plan before you start writing.

1. New ideas didn't = new treatments
   - Vesalius = better understanding of anatomy
   - Useful for surgeons but not physicians
2. People slow to accept new ideas
   - Miasma popular since ancient times
   - Miasma treatments seemed to work
3. Quality of medical instruments
   - Poor quality, e.g. microscopes
   - No proof for new theories

The best answers are well organised, with three paragraphs. Structure your plan to reflect this.

Keep your plan short and simple. You don't need to write in full sentences.

Number the points in your plan so you have an order for your answer.

Remember to include your own knowledge in the plan. This plan includes a third reason which was not mentioned in the question.

This is one style of plan. You can see another style on page 41.

Had a look ☐ **Nearly there** ☐ **Nailed it!** ☐

Answering Question 4

Steps to success

1 Write a paragraph about your first point. Remember to use PEEL to structure your paragraph clearly.

One reason that the change in the treatment of disease was very slow during the Renaissance was that, although there were new ideas and understanding, these did not affect treatment. For example, Andreas Vesalius dissected a large number of human bodies, and his detailed illustrations were published in England and throughout Europe. This improved understanding of how the human body worked and later helped surgeons, but not apothecaries and physicians. As a result, it was still difficult to diagnose and treat diseases. This meant that treatments stayed more or less the same.

Make a clear **point** at the start to show what the paragraph is about. This example uses one of the reasons given in the question.

Include some **evidence**. This example only uses a couple of points about Vesalius but it is enough to show understanding of the topic.

Explain how the reason caused the type of change (here, the slow change in treatment).

Link back to the question.

2 Write a paragraph about your second point. Keep focused on the question and use PEEL to structure your writing.

A second reason was that people were slow to accept new ideas. For example, the theory of miasma said that disease was caused by bad air and treatment included using birds in sick rooms to circulate the air. This theory had originated in the Ancient world and had been popular throughout the Middle Ages. As a result, by the Renaissance, people were used to this traditional idea and trusted it because it seemed to work. Consequently, because people stuck to familiar theories, they also stuck to their treatments, so there was not much change in how disease was treated.

Make a second **point**. You could use the other reason given in the question.

Give **evidence** to support your point.

Explain – here, the phrase 'as a result' is used to write analytically.

Link back to the question.

3 Write a paragraph about your third point. Remember to refer back to your plan and stay focused on explaining why.

A third reason was that the medical instruments that were available were not very good quality…

As a result…

This meant that the treatment of disease changed very slowly in the years c1500 to c1700 because…

Always include **three** reasons. This paragraph is about a reason that was not suggested in the question – so it also uses the student's own knowledge.

Had a look ☐ **Nearly there** ☐ **Nailed it!** ☐

Understanding Question 5/6

Question 5/6 will always be structured in the same way. Make sure you know how this question works and what it is asking you to do.

How does Question 5/6 work?

5/6 'The Church prevented progress in medicine in the Middle Ages.'

How far do you agree? Explain your answer.

(16 marks plus 4 marks for SPaG and use of specialist terminology)

You may use the following in your answer:

- Church control of education
- hospitals

You **must** also use information of your own.

Identify the command phrase – 'how far' means you need to make a judgement.

Check how many marks the question is worth – this will help you to manage your time.

Look at the two factors suggested – they might be helpful in deciding what to write about.

You **must** use your own information – this includes writing about at least one factor that is not given in the question.

Identify the opinion in the statement – this question will always start with an opinion about something.

Up to four of the marks of the total for this question will be awarded for good use of spelling, punctuation and grammar, and for use of specialist terminology.

You can find out about key terms and SPaG on pages 15 and 16.

You will have **a choice of two questions**. You must answer **either** Question 5 **or** Question 6. Both of them will be structured like this.

Links This question is similar to Question 1c on Paper 2 (your British depth study).

What does Question 5/6 assess?

- Question 5/6 tests Assessment Objectives 1 and 2.
- You need to show your knowledge of the topic.
- You also need to show you can explain and analyse events using second-order concepts such as causation and change.

How long should I spend?

Spend about 25 minutes on Question 5/6.

This question is worth more marks than any other question on your exam paper, so make sure you leave enough time to finish your answer.

Take a look at page 17 for more about the assessment objectives.

Analysing the statement

Make sure you understand the statement.

- Identify what the question is about – the example above is about the Church's impact on medicine in the Middle Ages.
- **Identify the opinion clearly** – in the example above, the opinion is that the Church prevented progress in medicine.

Choosing factors to write about

Question 5/6 will always include two bullet points. **These bullet points are only suggestions of factors you could use to support or challenge the statement – you don't have to use them.** If you don't know what one of the bullet points means, or you don't feel confident writing about it, you can choose to write about another factor.

Had a look ☐ **Nearly there** ☐ **Nailed it!** ☐

Understanding Question 5/6

'How far do you agree?'

You need to reach a judgement about the statement in the question.

- Look at evidence that agrees with the statement **and** at evidence that challenges it.
- Use your knowledge to reach an overall judgement – don't just write down everything you know about the topic.
- Explain why you have made that judgement.

Your overall judgement

Your overall judgement needs to be justified – you need to include a reason for your decision. In your overall judgement, make sure you:

- **Say how far you agree** with the statement – for example, 'Overall, I agree...'
- **Give a clear reason** for your opinion by comparing the factors in a short summary at the end of your answer.

How is Question 5/6 marked?

Strong answers to Question 5/6:

- ✓ give an analytical explanation which is tightly focused on the question throughout
- ✓ keep their explanation clear and well-organised throughout
- ✓ include information that is accurate, relevant and closely linked to the question
- ✓ show a wide range of knowledge and understanding of the topic
- ✓ reach an overall judgement which is fully justified
- ✓ use correct spelling, punctuation and grammar and specialist terms.

Writing analytically

Use phrases that show you are explaining the opinion in the statement and making a judgement about that viewpoint. This is called writing analytically. For example:

- I agree/do not agree...
- Although I agree to a certain extent... it is also true that...
- The viewpoint is valid because...
- This can be supported by...

Top tip

Remember to use **key terms** in your answer.

Turn to page 12 for more about writing clear answers. You can find examples of key terms on page 15.

You **will** need to write an introduction and conclusion for Question 5/6.

Top tips for success

Top tip

- ✓ **Plan** your answer before you write to help you to stay focused on the question.
- ✓ Start with a **short introduction** – say what you will cover in your answer.
- ✓ Include **arguments for the statement** in the question and **counter-arguments**.
- ✓ Use **clear and accurate evidence** to support your arguments.
- ✓ **Explain clearly why** your evidence supports or challenges the statement.
- ✓ **Link factors together and compare them** to say which is more important.
- ✓ Use **information of your own** – at least one factor not given in the question.
- ✓ Structure your answer clearly using **PEEL paragraphs**.
- ✓ If the question includes a date range (for example, 'since c1800') only include information from that period, and cover the whole period.
- ✓ Use correct **spelling, punctuation, grammar** and **specialist terminology**.
- ✓ End with an **overall judgement** about how far you agree with the statement.

Had a look ☐ **Nearly there** ☐ **Nailed it!** ☐

Answering Question 5/6

You need to understand how you can write a successful answer to Question 5/6.

Reading the question

> **5/6** 'The Church prevented progress in medicine in the Middle Ages.'
>
> How far do you agree? Explain your answer.
>
> **(16 marks plus 4 marks for SPaG and use of specialist terminology)**
>
> You may use the following in your answer:
>
> - Church control of education
> - hospitals
>
> You **must** also use information of your own.

Always read the question carefully before you start writing your answer.

Make sure you identify the opinion in the statement.

Remember that up to four marks are available for the quality of your writing.

Use **PEEL** paragraphs.
See page 12 for more about paragraphing and PEEL.

How can I structure my answer?

1. Write a short introduction. Say what the question is about and what you will write about.
2. Begin your argument. You could start by writing about evidence that supports the statement.
3. Continue your argument. If you started with evidence that supports the statement, move on to write about other factors that challenge the statement.
4. Write a conclusion. Give an overall judgement and explain why you reached that decision.

Plan your answer

This question is worth 16 marks, so take the time to make a good plan before you start writing.

Support	Challenge
1. Church control of education • Controlled unis where physicians trained • Only monks + priests could read 2. Discouraged new ideas • Dissection not allowed • Disease = God's will	1. Hospitals • Jesus' example = caring for sick • Most Church run and funded 2. Church teachings advised keeping clean, fresh food, rest, etc
Judgement: Mostly agree – some positive impact but Church mostly prevented progress	

List factors that support and challenge the statement.

Include specific evidence.

Include your own knowledge. This factor was not mentioned in the question.

Include a judgement to help you stay focused.

Had a look ☐ **Nearly there** ☐ **Nailed it!** ☐

Answering Question 5/6

Steps to success

1 Write a short introduction. Say what the question is about and what you will write about.

The Church both helped and prevented progress in medicine in the Middle Ages. For example, the Church funded and ran most hospitals which improved medicine but also controlled education and therefore only taught ideas it approved of, which prevented progress. Despite some improvements, however, I think the Church did mostly prevent progress.

Identify what the question is about. Use words from the statement.

Indicate the viewpoints that you will cover.

Making a judgement here will help to focus your answer.

2 Begin your argument. You could start by writing about evidence that supports the statement.

Education was almost totally controlled by the Church during the Middle Ages. Oxford and Cambridge universities, where physicians were trained, were set up and run by the Church. The only learning most people received was from priests during church services. Apart from priests and monks, few people could read and write. As most large collections of books were in monasteries, the only books available were ones that were approved by the Church. Consequently, people were only taught ideas the Church approved. As most of these ideas were incorrect, this prevented progress in medicine....

Use clear language to identify the **point**.

Use your knowledge to give **specific evidence**.

Explain how your evidence supports your point. Here, the word 'Consequently' is used to write analytically.

Link back to the question.

3 Continue your argument. Once you have given all the evidence that supports the statement, move on to write about other factors – as in this example.

However, although I mostly agree with the viewpoint in the statement, there were areas where the Church helped progress in medicine. For example, the Church taught people to keep clean and advised people to eat fresh food and rest when they were unwell....

Always include a **counter-argument** – even if you agree with the statement. Signpost it clearly.

Use phrases that show you are making a judgement.

Include information that is not included in the question, like this.

4 Write a conclusion. Give an overall judgement about how far you agree with the statement.

Overall, I mostly agree with the statement. Although the Church did help in areas such as healthy living and caring for the sick, it controlled education and discouraged new ideas, so there was very little progress in the treatment or prevention of disease. Consequently, the Church largely did prevent progress in medicine in the Middle Ages.

Give your overall judgement on the statement. You could also start with 'In conclusion...'

Explain your overall judgement by comparing the factors you have considered.

Had a look ☐ **Nearly there** ☐ **Nailed it!** ☐

This is how long you have to answer all the questions for your Paper 1 thematic study and historic environment in the exam.

In the exam, the sources you need are in a separate booklet. Here, you can find the sources on page 61.

Get used to writing with a black pen.

In the exam, there will be spaces for you to do this.

Check carefully which questions you **must** answer, and where you have a choice.

Focus on answering each question fully, rather than trying to fill all the writing lines.

Use the marks to help you work out how long to spend on each question.

Pearson Edexcel GCSE (9–1)

History

Paper 1: Thematic study and historic environment

Option 11: Medicine in Britain, c1250–present *and*

The British sector of the Western Front, 1914–18: injuries, treatment and the trenches

Time: 1 hour 15 minutes

You must have: Sources Booklet

Instructions

- Use **black ink** or ball-point pen.
- **Fill in** your name, centre number and candidate number.
- There are two sections in this question paper. Answer Questions 1 and 2 from Section A. From Section B, answer Questions 3 and 4 and then **EITHER** Question 5 **OR** Question 6.
- Answer the questions in the spaces provided – there may be more space than you need.

Information

- The total mark for this paper is 52.
- The marks for **each** question are shown in brackets.
- The marks available for spelling, punctuation, grammar and use of specialist terminology are clearly indicated.

In Paper 1, it is Question 5/6 that has additional marks available for SPaG and use of specialist terminology.

Top tip

Make sure you:

- read each question carefully before you start writing your answer
- try to answer every question
- save about five minutes to check your answers at the end.

SECTION A: The British sector of the Western Front, 1914–18: injuries, treatment and the trenches
Answer Questions 1 and 2.

Describe **two** features of x-ray machines used on the Western Front.

(4 marks)

Feature 1

one feature become smaller and easier to move.

Feature 2

One feature is over time the ~~ex~~ x-rays got better as before theradiology was so strong it could burn hair off.

Time

Spend **about 5 minutes** on this question.

Unlocking the question

A **feature** means any relevant, accurate piece of information about the question topic.

Unlocking the question

Describing means giving information about the question topic. You don't need to give reasons or say how important it was.

Revision Guide

Revise this topic on pages 27–28.

Watch out!

Make sure you describe **two different features.**

LEARN IT!

Use phrases like 'One feature was…' to make your answer clear.

Hint

Add **relevant supporting information** to each feature.

Hint

Use key terms to show your topic knowledge.

Top tip

Keep your answer specific, accurate and concise.

Time

Spend **about 14 minutes** on this question.

Top tip

Note down a **quick** plan. Include points you will make for each source.

Revision Guide

Revise this topic on pages 25 and 28.

Unlocking the question

You need to make a judgement about **how useful** each source is **for the enquiry** in the question.

Unlocking the question

You must refer to **both sources** and use your **own knowledge** in your answer.

Unlocking the question

Usefulness is about what the source tells you about the enquiry and how accurate it is.

Unlocking the question

You need to consider both the **content** and **provenance** of each source and **explain** why this makes the source more or less useful.

Top tip

Structure your answer clearly. Write about one source, then the other.

2a Study Sources A and B on page 61.

How useful are Sources A and B for an enquiry into the effectiveness of medical treatment on the Western Front?

Explain your answer, using Sources A and B and your knowledge of the historical context.

(8 marks)

- figures
- cases
- how busy
- how many people were there.
- what they looked like.
- what would happen
- dates
- Sanitary (cattle-truck)
- how many nurses and doctors.

LEARN IT!

Remember: provenance is **nature**, **origin** and **purpose**.

Watch out!

Make sure you stay focused on the enquiry in the question.

Watch out!

You don't need to compare the sources or decide which one is more useful.

Hint

Compare the source with your **own knowledge**. Does the source support what you know?

Hint

A source which is **accurate and balanced** is usually more useful than one that is exaggerated and one-sided.

Watch out!

Don't say a source is useless – no source in the exam will ever be useless for the enquiry.

LEARN IT!

Use phrases such as 'not very useful', and 'very useful' to show your opinion of each source.

Hint

Think about whether the information in the source is **accurate**. Is it balanced?

Time

Spend **about 5 minutes** on this question.

Unlocking the question

The question will only ask about **one** source. Look at the right one.

Unlocking the question

The enquiry in this question will always be the same as the enquiry in Question 2a.

Hint

Use the table to help keep your answer concise.

Hint

Choose **one** detail from the source that is **specific** and **relevant to the enquiry** in the question.

Top tip

If it's a written source, **quote** a detail from it.

Watch out!

Your follow-up question **must** be linked to the detail you have identified **and** the enquiry.

Hint

The type of source must help to answer your follow-up question and must be **specific**.

Watch out!

Your explanation must be **precise**.

2b Study Source A on page 61.

How could you follow up Source A to find out more about the effectiveness of medical treatment on the Western Front?

In your answer, you must give the question you would ask and the type of source you could use.

Complete the table below.

(4 marks)

Detail in Source A that I would follow up:

1st line in source.

Question I would ask:

how meny casulitie did red cr worker heve dealt with

What type of source I could use:

causlty clearing records.

How this might help answer my question:

record give numbers of casoultie.

SECTION B: Medicine in Britain, c1250–present

Answer Questions 3 and 4. Then answer EITHER Question 5 OR 6.

Explain **one** way in which medical training for physicians in the medieval period (c1250–c1500) was different from medical training for physicians in the Renaissance (c1500–c1700).

(4 marks)

....

....

....

....

....

....

....

....

....

....

....

....

....

....

....

....

Time

Spend **about 5 minutes** on this question.

Unlocking the question

You need to provide details of **one** way in which something was **similar/ different** across two different time periods.

Unlocking the question

You will always be asked **either** about a similarity **or** about a difference.

Revision Guide

Revise this topic on pages 1, 4 and 9.

Top tip

State the difference/ similarity clearly at the **beginning** of your answer.

Watch out!

Make sure your difference/ similarity is linked to the topic in the question.

Watch out!

Focus on **how** it was different, not why.

Hint

Make your supporting information balanced – give examples for **each** time period.

Watch out!

Keep your examples **specific** and **relevant** to your difference/similarity.

Time

Spend **about 18 minutes** on this question.

Top tip

Always start 12-mark questions with a quick plan. Use the Notes pages at the back of this book if you need extra space – but keep your plan **short**.

Unlocking the question

The command phrase in this question will always be 'Explain why' so you will always have to **give reasons** for something happening or not happening.

Unlocking the question

The bullet points give you suggestions on what to write about, but you don't have to use them if you don't want to.

Unlocking the question

You **must** include at least one reason from your own knowledge.

Revision Guide

Revise this topic on pages 15–17.

Hint

Start your paragraphs with phrases like 'One reason is...', 'A second reason is...' and so on, to make your answer clear.

4 Explain why there was progress in the prevention of disease between c1700 and c1900.

(12 marks)

You may use the following in your answer:

- Jenner's smallpox vaccination
- Public Health Act 1875

You **must** also use information of your own.

Practice paper

Hint

You don't need to write an introduction or a conclusion for this answer.

Watch out!

You **must** stick to the date range given in the question.

Hint

Support each reason with **clear and accurate information** about the topic.

Watch out!

You **don't** have to decide which reason was more important.

Aim higher

Make sure your explanation is analytical, and keep it tightly focused on the question throughout your answer.

Hint

Use **key terms**, like names, dates or specific examples, to support each reason you give.

LEARN IT!

Structure your answer clearly. Use a separate **PEEL (Point – Evidence – Explain – Link)** paragraph to write about each reason.

LEARN IT!

Use phrases like 'as a result…', 'consequently…' or 'this caused…' to focus your answer and show you are writing **analytically**.

Top tip

You need to include **three** reasons in your answer and each one needs to be connected to the question topic.

Watch out!

Make sure that you are **giving reasons** for the issue in the question, not just describing the topic. You need to say clearly why each reason you give caused the change in the question.

Answer EITHER Question 5 OR Question 6.
Spelling, punctuation, grammar and use of specialist terminology will be assessed in this question.

:ITHER

'Florence Nightingale's work is the most important reason why there were improvements in hospital treatment and care between c1700 and c1900.'

How far do you agree? Explain your answer.

(16 marks plus 4 marks for SPaG and use of specialist terminology)

You may use the following in your answer:

- training for nurses
- the development of antiseptics

You **must** also use information of your own.

)R

'The development of penicillin is the most important breakthrough in the treatment of disease since c1800.'

How far do you agree? Explain your answer.

(16 marks plus 4 marks for SPaG and use of specialist terminology)

You may use the following in your answer:

- Alexander Fleming, Howard Florey and Ernst Chain
- high-tech treatments

You **must** also use information of your own.

Time

Remember that this question is worth more marks than the other questions on your thematic study. Make sure you leave enough time to answer it fully.

Watch out!

In the exam, you only need to answer **one** of these questions. Don't try to answer both!

Unlocking the question

Look carefully at each question, including the suggestions in the bullet points, and consider how much you know about each topic. Choose the question you feel you can write most about.

Top tip

It is worth spending a short time carefully choosing the question before you start writing. This way you are more likely to pick the question you can answer best, which will save you time overall.

Revision Guide

For Question 5, revise improvements in hospital treatment and care between c1700 and c1900 on page 13.

Revision Guide

For Question 6, revise breakthroughs in the treatment of disease since c1800 on pages 20 and 22–23.

Watch out!

In the exam, you should only answer **either** Question 5 **or** Question 6. In this practice paper there is space for you to have a go at both options.

Hint

Use this space to answer Question 5.

Time

Spend **about 25 minutes** on this question.

Top tip

Always start 16-mark questions with a good plan.

Unlocking the question

You need to reach a **clear judgement** in your answer.

Unlocking the question

Identify the opinion in the question before you start writing. Make sure you know what you need to reach a judgement about.

Aim higher

State your judgement in a short introduction – this will help you to keep your answer focused.

Unlocking the question

You **must** include **at least one factor** that is not mentioned in the question.

Indicate which question you are answering by marking a cross in the box ☒. If you change your mind, put a line through the box ~~☒~~ and then indicate you new question with a cross ☒.

Chosen question number:

Question 5 ☒

Question 6 ☒

....

....

....

....

....

....

....

....

....

....

....

....

....

....

....

....

....

....

....

....

....

....

....

....

....

....

....

....

Top tip

Structure your answer clearly. Either start by writing about information that supports the statement, or information that challenges it.

Unlocking the question

You don't have to use the two bullet points, but they might help you decide what to write about.

Unlocking the question

It doesn't matter whether you agree or disagree with the statement – you still need to consider evidence that supports the statement **and** evidence that challenges it.

Unlocking the question

This question assesses your **spelling, punctuation, grammar** and **use of specialist terms**.

Watch out!

Don't just give your opinion. Make sure you **explain** why you have reached your judgement.

Top tip

Use PEEL **(Point – Evidence – Explain – Link)** paragraphs to organise each main point.

Hint

Link each point of evidence to the question. Use phrases like 'this shows that…'

Watch out!

Avoid making statements that are too general. Use **specific and accurate** examples.

Hint

Each point you make should clearly support or challenge the statement in the question.

Watch out!

Make sure you stick to the **time period** the question is asking about.

LEARN IT!

Use phrases that show you are **explaining** the viewpoint and making a **judgement** about it – such as 'The viewpoint is valid because…'

Watch out!

Don't just describe the topic. Be clear about **how** your examples support or challenge the statement.

Hint

Use **key terms** to show your topic knowledge and understanding.

LEARN IT!

Practise any spellings you find tricky. This will help you to write an answer that is strong in SPaG.

Aim higher

Link the factors together. One place to do this is in the conclusion.

Aim higher

Compare the factors to show which are more important, or which had an impact on other factors.

Hint

Your conclusion must reach a **clear judgement**.

Hint

You could start your conclusion with 'Overall, I...' or 'In conclusion...'

Watch out!

You need to state how far you agree with the statement **and** explain why you have reached this judgement.

Top tip

To explain your judgement clearly, think about **why** you have reached that opinion. For example, did one factor have more effect than other factors?

Watch out!

In the exam, you should only answer **either** Question 5 **or** Question 6. In this practice paper there is space for you to have a go at both options.

Hint

Use this space to answer Question 6.

Time

Spend **about 25 minutes** on this question.

Top tip

Always start 16-mark questions with a good plan. Use the Notes pages at the back of this book if you need extra space.

Unlocking the question

Identify the opinion in the question before you start writing. Make sure you know what you need to reach a judgement about.

Hint

Start with an **introduction** – give a short summary of what you are going to write about.

Aim higher

Decide on your judgement before you start writing. This will help you to write a more focused **analytical** explanation.

Indicate which question you are answering by marking a cross in the box ☒. If you change your mind, put a line through the box ☒ and then indicate your new question with a cross ☒.

Chosen question number:

Question 5 ☒

Question 6 ☒

....

....

....

....

....

....

....

....

....

....

....

....

....

....

....

....

....

....

....

....

....

....

....

....

....

....

....

Unlocking the question

Look at the two bullet points. They will help you decide what to include in your answer.

Unlocking the question

You **must** include at least one factor that is not mentioned in the question.

Unlocking the question

You need to consider evidence that supports the statement **and** evidence that challenges it.

Unlocking the question

Pay attention to the **quality of your writing** for this answer. This question has additional marks available for SPaG and use of specialist terms.

Top tip

Structure your answer clearly. Either start by writing about information that supports the statement, or information that challenges it.

Aim higher

You don't need to wait until the conclusion to show your judgement. As you write about a factor, use phrases like 'this was more/less important because...' to explain your viewpoint.

Hint

Once you have written about your evidence that supports or challenges the statement, write your **counter-argument**.

Top tip

Use PEEL **(Point – Evidence – Explain – Link)** paragraphs to organise each main point.

Watch out!

Stay focused. **Link** each point of evidence back to the question to avoid going off the topic.

Aim higher

Include **specific, accurate details** to back up each main point – for example, details of people, events and dates.

Top tip

As you write, look back at the question occasionally. This will help you to stay focused on the question.

Watch out!

Make sure you stick to the **time period** the question is asking about.

Top tip

Start each paragraph with **clear language** that focuses what you are writing. For example, you could write 'Another example that supports/challenges the statement is...'

....

....

....

....

....

....

....

....

....

....

....

....

....

....

....

....

....

....

....

....

....

....

....

....

....

....

....

....

....

....

....

....

....

....

Watch out!

You need to **explain why** your evidence supports or challenges the statement. Don't just describe what you know.

LEARN IT!

Use phrases that show you are **explaining** the viewpoint and **making a judgement** about it – such as 'The viewpoint is valid because...', 'However, it is also true that...', 'This can be supported by...'

LEARN IT!

Practise tricky spellings and get used to starting and ending your sentences clearly. This will help you to write an answer that is strong in SPaG.

Hint

Always finish Question 5/6 with a conclusion that gives an **overall judgement** that is fully justified.

Hint

You could start your conclusion with 'Overall, I...' or 'In conclusion...'

Top tip

Double-check your conclusion. What reason have you given for your judgement? Make sure it is **clear and specific**.

Sources for use with Section A.

Source A: Extracts from a diary written in 1914 by a nursing sister who spent most of her time on ambulance trains and casualty clearing stations.

Sunday, September 20th

Three trains full of wounded, numbering altogether 1175 cases, have been dressed at the station today; we were sent down at 11 this morning. The train I was put to had 510 cases. You boarded a cattle-truck, armed with a tray of dressings and a pail; the men were lying on straw; had been in trains for several days; most had only been dressed once, and many were gangrenous. If you found one urgently needed amputation or operation or was likely to die, you called an M.O. to have him taken off the train for Hospital.... The platform was soon packed with stretchers with all the bad cases waiting patiently to be taken to Hospital. ... They were nearly all shrapnel shell wounds – more ghastly than anything I have ever seen or smelt...

Tuesday, September 22nd

When we got back this morning, nine of those we took off the trains on Sunday afternoon had died here, and one before reaching the hospital – three of tetanus. I haven't heard how many at the other hospital at the Jesuit school – tetanus there too. Some of the amputations die of septic absorption and shock, and you wouldn't wonder if you saw them...

Source B: A photograph showing a ward at a base hospital on the Western Front in June 1917. The patient nearest the camera seems to be having his leg wound treated with sterilised salt solution.

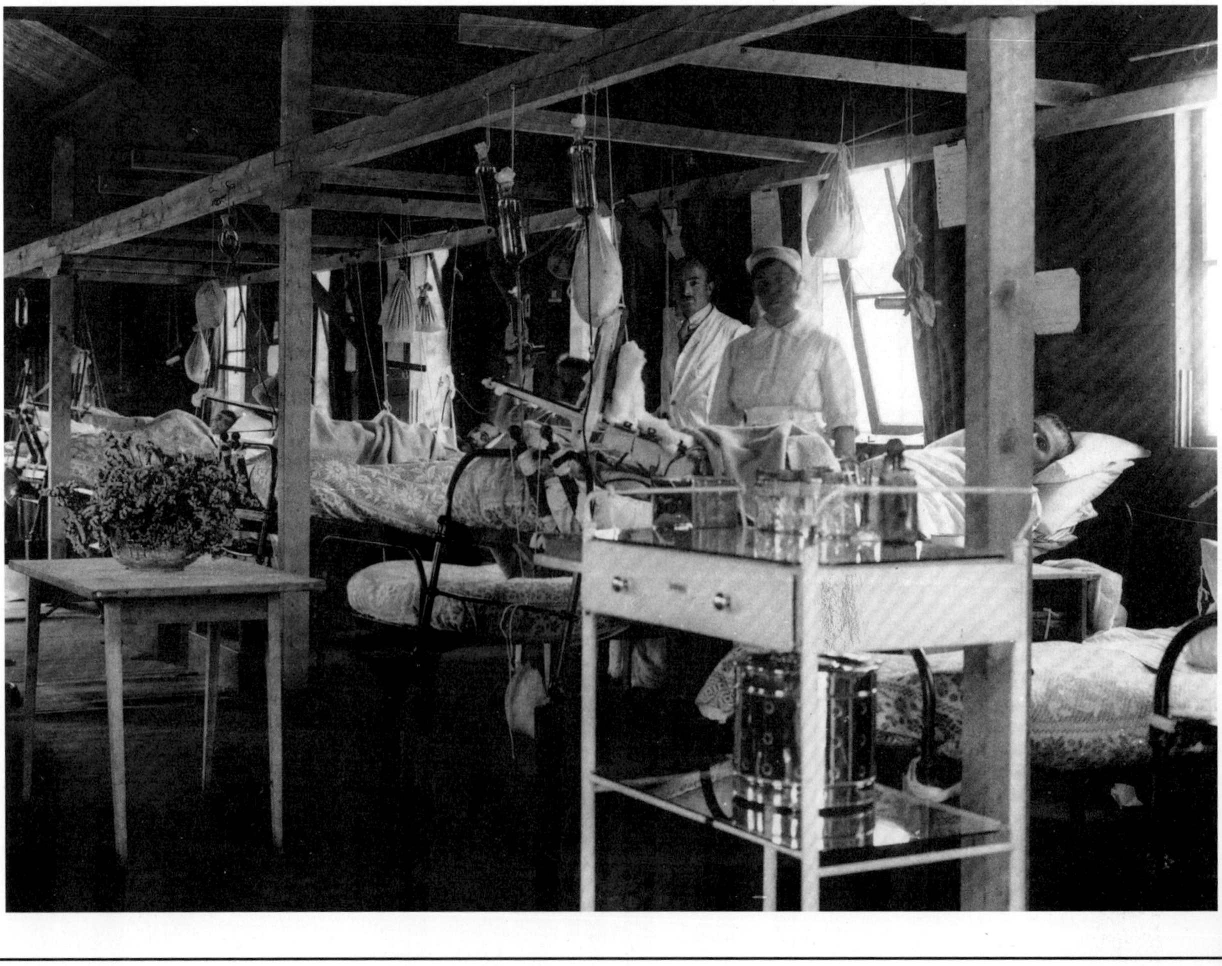

SECTION A: The British sector of the Western Front, 1914–18: injuries, treatment and the trenches

Answer Questions 1 and 2.

Describe **two** features of x-ray machines used on the Western Front.

(4 marks)

Feature 1

One feature was that some small, mobile x-ray machines could be used close to the front line. The images were fuzzy but they still gave an idea of how serious injuries were.

Feature 2

A second feature was that larger, more accurate x-ray machines were used in field hospitals. These machines enabled accurate diagnosis and allowed surgery to be carried out accurately and quickly.

This is a valid feature.

Supporting information gives more detail about the feature.

Answer is kept concise with specific and accurate examples given.

Each feature is written in the space provided.

Second feature is different to the first and is also valid.

Second feature is also developed with accurate supporting information.

ternative answers

nswers to Question 1 could also include:

Mobile x-ray machines were lighter than static units. **(1)** This meant they could be used closer to the front line. **(1)**

X-ray machines were vital for successful treatment of many injuries. **(1)** They showed the precise location of bullets and shrapnel which helped successfully remove them from the body. **(1)**

X-ray machines were improved and developed as the war went on. **(1)** The x-ray machines available in 1914 were very large and heavy so could not be easily moved, so smaller, mobile units were developed. **(1)**

Hint

Turn to page 61 to remind yourself about Sources A and B.

Hint

Read the notes below, then look at the sample answer on page 64.

2a Study Sources A and B on page 61.

How useful are Sources A and B for an enquiry into the effectiveness of medical treatment on the Western Front?

Explain your answer, using Sources A and B and your knowledge of the historical context.

(8 marks

Writing a good answer

Good answers will:

- judge the usefulness of each source for the enquiry given in the question
- explain clearly how the provenance of each source makes it more or less useful
- support judgements with comments on the content and the provenance of each source
- use own knowledge to interpret the sources and support their judgements.

Relevant points about Source A may include:

- The descriptions of the nature of the injuries and the typical outcomes, such as amputation, tetanus or deat help to show how available treatments were not able to cope.
- The source is useful because it gives details of treatments that are very basic and therefore not very effect
- The source is a personal diary extract so is unlikely to be exaggerated and is probably a reliable record.
- The diary entry is from 1914 so only gives information about the beginning of the war.

Relevant points about Source B may include:

- The photograph shows the Carrel-Dakin method in use, which suggests that it was being used to prevent infections from spreading.
- The photograph only shows the Carrel-Dakin method in use for one patient and we do not know if that patie survived.
- The photograph should be an accurate record of the treatments being used but the scene looks as though might have been staged.
- The fact that the Carrel-Dakin method seems to be the focus of the photograph suggests that it was considered effective.

Q2a: sample answer

Plan:

Source A	Source B
• Basic treatment – large no. of infections • I know treatments in 1914 = quite basic, esp. for infection • Diary – personal so not exaggerated • Very useful	• Shows Carrel-Dakin method • I know this method = effective + used later in war • Photo – not faked but poss. staged • Quite useful

Source A is very useful for an enquiry into the effectiveness of medical treatment on the Western Front because it describes how the wounded were treated on trains, lying in straw, and how most wounds 'had only been dressed once' before this, which highlights how basic the treatment was. It also describes how 'ghastly' the wounds were and says 'many were gangrenous'. The source suggests that treatment was not very effective and this supports what I know which is that wound infections caused by bacteria like gas gangrene and tetanus were very common and often led to death due to the unhygienic conditions on the Western Front in 1914. Source A is an extract from a nurse's diary, so it was probably written as a personal record, or for family or friends to read. As a result, it is likely to give an accurate picture because the nurse would have no reason to exaggerate. The writer is a nursing sister so she was experienced and well qualified which means the description is probably reliable. However, this extract was written in 1914, so it only gives information about the beginning of the war, and not how things developed. Source A is still very useful, however, because it shows the challenges of giving medical treatment on the Western Front in 1914.

Quick plan helps to make answer clear and focused.

Answer looks at one source at a time, giving clear structure.

Begins with clear judgement about first source.

Analyses content of first source, staying focused on enquiry topic.

Short quotations used to support points.

Compares source content to own knowledge.

Analyses provenance of first source and explains effect on usefulness.

Finishes analysis of first source with overall judgement about its usefulness.

Hint

Look at this sample answer to Question 2a. Refer back to the notes on page 63, then look to see how some of the points are used here.

Content and provenance of second source analysed.

Language used shows focus on giving clear judgement.

Use of key terms shows strong knowledge of topic.

Uses own knowledge to explain how source content fits with enquiry topic.

Considers accuracy of source and how this affects usefulness.

Gives clear reason for overall judgement about second source.

Source B is quite useful because it shows a soldier being treated using the Carrel-Dakin method. This involved moving sterilised salt solution through a wound using tubes in order to make and keep the wound sterile and stop infections from developing and spreading. The photograph shows bottles with clear liquid hanging above the patient's foot and tubes leading towards his leg, so these details support what I know. I know that this method was developed because so many of the wounded were dying from infection early in the war. It was found to be effective in stopping infection so was often used later in the war, which is supported by the fact that it is being used here in June 1917. Source B is a photograph taken at a base hospital on the Western Front in June 1917 so it is probably a fairly accurate picture of what treatments at this time involved. However, it might have been staged, as everything looks very tidy and there are even flowers. Also, the only patient with the salt solution is the one nearest the camera and we don't know if he survived. Although it is possible that the Carrel-Dakin method was not used more widely in this ward, the fact that it is the focus of the photograph suggests it was considered effective, which makes the source quite useful overall.

A very strong answer because...

This answer makes a clear judgement about the usefulness of each source. The content of the sources is analysed and compared to the student's own knowledge. The student also considers the provenance of each source and explains how this affects its usefulness. Relevant examples from the sources are used as evidence. The structure of the answer is clear, with one source analysed first and then the other. Starting with a quick p has helped the student to keep their answer tightly focused on the question throughout.

b Study Source A on page 61.

How could you follow up Source A to find out more about the effectiveness of medical treatment on the Western Front?

In your answer, you must give the question you would ask and the type of source you could use.

Complete the table below.

(4 marks)

Detail in Source A that I would follow up:

'Three trains full of wounded, numbering altogether 1175 cases, have been dressed at the station today'

Question I would ask:

How many casualties did each medical worker have to deal with at casualty clearing stations?

What type of source I could use:

Casualty clearing station records

How this might help answer my question:

These records should give numbers of casualties treated each day and the number of medical workers treating them. This could be added up and divided to find an average.

Hint

Turn to page 61 to remind yourself about Source A.

Answer kept concise.

Detail chosen is specific, relevant to the enquiry and from the source itself, not the provenance.

Uses direct quotation from the source.

Follow-up question linked to the detail selected from source and the enquiry in the question.

Answer space used correctly, making answer clear.

Type of source selected is specific and relates to follow-up question given.

Precise explanation of how the type of source chosen would help to answer the follow-up question.

ernative nswers

other answer to Question 2b might be:

Detail in Source A that I would follow up: 'nine of those we took off the trains on Sunday afternoon had died here, and one before reaching the hospital – three of tetanus'. **(1)**

Question I would ask: How many soldiers died from wound infections rather than wounds themselves? **(1)**

What type of source I would look for: Base hospital records. **(1)**

How this might help answer my question: These should record what different patients died from. **(1)**

Hint

Read the notes below, then look at the sample answer that follows.

SECTION B: Medicine in Britain, c1250–present
Answer Questions 3 and 4. Then answer EITHER Question 5 OR 6.

3 Explain **one** way in which medical training for physicians in the medieva period (c1250–c1500) was different from medical training for physicians i the Renaissance (c1500–c1700).

(4 mark

Writing a good answer

Good answers will:

- analyse features of the period to explain a difference or similarity
- give specific information about the topic to support the comparison
- show good knowledge and understanding of both time periods.

Relevant points may include:

- In the medieval period, medical training was controlled by the Church, whereas during the Renaissance the Church had far less control, which meant students had access to more ideas.
- In the medieval period, all training was through reading books; in the Renaissance, training began to include practical experiments, including dissection.

Hint

Look at this sample answer to Question 3. Refer back to the notes above, then look to see how some of the points are used here.

Q3: sample answer

One way in which medical training for physicians was different is that in the medieval period the Church had more control over the training than it did during the Renaissance.

For example, in the medieval period, people training to be physicians were only taught from books that the Church approved of. These book included ideas such as the Theory of the Four Humours and Galen's Theory of Opposites.

In comparison, in the Renaissance, the Church had little control over what books were published so students had access to a wider variety of ideas. For example, students were taught human anatomy from the detailed drawings in Andreas Vesalius' books.

Difference clearly stated.

Difference linked to topic in question.

Difference explained with examples from each period.

Key terms show strong understanding of topic.

Language shows time periods are being compared.

Examples are relevant, specific and accurate.

A very strong answer because...

The student identifies and clearly states one difference between the two time periods. The difference is link to the question topic. The answer stays focused on analysing and explaining how it was different by giving specific, relevant and accurate examples from each period. Both time periods are given equal attention.

Explain why there was progress in the prevention of disease between c1700 and c1900.

(12 marks)

You may use the following in your answer:

- Jenner's smallpox vaccination
- Public Health Act 1875

You **must** also use information of your own.

Hint

Read the notes below, then look at the sample answer that follows.

Writing a good answer

Good answers will:

- give an analytical explanation which is tightly focused on the question throughout
- keep the explanation clear and well organised throughout
- include information that is accurate, relevant and closely linked to the question
- show a wide range of knowledge and understanding of the topic.

Relevant points may include:

- Jenner's use of scientific methods proved that the smallpox vaccine worked and helped prevent smallpox.
- As Jenner published his findings and included instructions for other doctors, awareness of the vaccination spread and in time was used more widely.
- John Snow's mapping of deaths in the Soho cholera epidemic of 1854 showed a strong link between contaminated water and the disease.
- John Snow had no scientific proof of his theory so people, including the government, didn't accept it immediately.
- The Public Health Act of 1875 made it compulsory for local councils to provide clean water and remove sewage, which reduced instances of water-borne diseases such as cholera.
- The Public Health Act of 1875 improved housing conditions, which reduced outbreaks of diseases such as tuberculosis.

Q4: sample answer

Hint

Look at this sample answer to Question 4. Refer back to the notes above, then look to see how some of the points are used here.

Plan:

1. Jenner's smallpox vaccination
   - J's scientific methods proved vaccination worked
   - J published findings + instructions – killer disease now preventable
2. John Snow's work
   - Showed link between dirty water + cholera
   - Fewer deaths from cholera + water supplies cleaned up
3. Public Health Act, 1875
   - Cities to provide clean water + remove sewage = fewer water-borne diseases, e.g. cholera
   - Higher housing standards = fewer diseases linked to damp, e.g. TB

Quick plan helps to keep answer clear and focused.

PEEL (Point – Evidence – Explain – Link) used to give clear structure in every paragraph.

Clear focus on time period given in question.

Relevant and accurate information used as evidence to support point.

One reason why there was progress in the prevention of disease between c1700 and c1900 was Jenner's smallpox vaccination. Jenner had noticed that people he had treated for cowpox never caught smallpox. He used scientific methods to carry out, record and repeat experiments which involved deliberately infecting people with cowpox and then trying to infect them with smallpox. As a result, Jenner was able to prove that this new method, which he called 'vaccination', worked. He published his findings, which included instructions other doctors could follow and which helped to spread awareness. Consequently, although this method only worked for smallpox and took time to become popular, it was now possible to prevent a common killer disease.

Three reasons given overall – including this one from own knowledge.

Use of key term shows strong knowledge of topic.

Shows accurate and relevant knowledge and understanding of the topic.

Language used to show writing is analytical – shows answer is explaining why.

A second reason was the work of John Snow which helped prevent people from catching cholera. In 1854, Snow mapped all the deaths in the cholera epidemic in Soho. He realised that the deaths were near to the Broad Street pump, so he removed the pump handle so that people couldn't collect water from it. This led to a dramatic fall in the number of deaths from cholera and seemed to show a clear link betwee contaminated water and the disease. Although Snow had no scientific evidence, and it took some time for his theory to be believed, by the mid-1860s it was generally accepted. This encouraged others to clean up their water supplies, which led to more progress in the prevention of disease.

Answer tightly focused on question throughout.

Each reason clearly signposted, making whole answer well organised.

A third reason was the Public Health Act of 1875. This act made city authorities provide clean water, sewers and public toilets. It also included laws about the quality of housing. For example, rented houses had to be inspected for cleanliness and new houses had to meet certain standards which would reduce damp and overcrowding. As a result, outbreaks of water-borne diseases such as cholera decreased and the last ever cholera epidemic in Britain took place in 1866–67. Outbreaks of diseases such as tuberculosis, which were spread in damp, overcrowded living conditions, were also reduced. Consequently, the Public Health Act of 1875, which involved the government taking responsibility to improve living conditions, led to real progress in the prevention of disease.

Explains why the reason caused the consequence in the question.

Specific detail shows wide range of topic knowledge.

Links back to the question.

A very strong answer because...

The answer provides a good explanation and stays focused on causation – for each point, the student provides relevant and accurate supporting evidence, then explains how this led to progress in the prevention of disease. Analytical language such as 'As a result...', 'This led to...' and 'Consequently...' shows the student is linking each reason back to the question. The answer is well structured, with clear PEEL paragraphs, which keeps the answer tightly focused on the question and makes it easy to follow.

Hint

Read the notes below, then look at the sample answer on page 72.

Hint

Remember – in the exam you only need to answer **either** Question 5 **or** Question 6.

Answer EITHER Question 5 OR Question 6.
Spelling, punctuation, grammar and use of specialist terminology will be assessed in this question.

5 'Florence Nightingale's work is the most important reason why there were improvements in hospital treatment and care between c1700 and c1900.'

How far do you agree? Explain your answer.

(16 marks plus 4 marks for SPaG and use of specialist terminology)

You may use the following in your answer:

- training for nurses
- the development of antiseptics

You **must** also use information of your own.

Writing a good answer

Good answers will:

- give an analytical explanation which is tightly focused on the question throughout
- keep explanations clear and well-organised throughout
- include information that is accurate, relevant and closely linked to the question
- show a wide range of knowledge and understanding of the topic
- reach an overall judgement which is fully justified
- use correct spelling, punctuation and grammar and specialist terms.

Relevant points that support the statement may include:

- Nightingale's work led to improvements in nursing care and made nursing a respectable profession.
- The Nightingale School for Nurses led the way in training for nurses.
- Nightingale improved organisation in hospitals, including the use of separate wards to stop the spread of infectious diseases.
- Before 1850, hospital conditions were generally very poor, but conditions later improved following Nightingale's focus on hygiene.

Relevant points to counter the statement may include:

- Joseph Lister introduced carbolic acid as the first antiseptic to prevent infection during surgery.
- Lister published his ideas, which led to the development of other antiseptics and aseptic techniques, which were used in hospitals by 1900.
- In the 18th and 19th centuries, charities opened more hospitals, which improved access to hospital care, especially outside London.
- Later in the 19th century, some specialist hospitals opened, such as asylums for the mentally ill and fever houses for infectious disease.

Q5: sample answer

Plan:

Support	Challenge
1. Nurses' training • Nursing became good profession • 'Notes on Nursing' + Nightingale School for Nurses 2. Improved hygiene • FN belief in miasma = more cleanliness • Better hygiene = less infection	3. Dev. of antiseptics • Lister + carbolic acid • Led to antiseptic + aseptic conditions in hospitals = less infection
Judgement: Disagree – FN work important but not as important as antiseptics + aseptic conditions	

Although Florence Nightingale's work is an important reason for improvements in hospital treatment and care between c1700 and c1900, I do not agree that Nightingale's work is the most important reason for the improvements. I think the development of antiseptic and then aseptic conditions is a more important reason for improvements in treatment and care, because it hugely reduced infection which had previously caused many deaths.

Florence Nightingale's work in the mid-1800s was very significant in improving training for nurses and this also improved nursing care in hospitals. Before Nightingale, nursing was not seen as a respectable profession for women and nurses had a reputation for being drunk and uncaring. Nightingale helped to change this because she was from a wealthy family, which encouraged more middle-class women to become nurses and nursing became a more popular job. Most significantly, she wrote 'Notes on Nursing' and set up the Nightingale School for Nurses. Before this, nurses received very little training, so her work vastly improved training for nurses. This helped change nursing into a respectable profession which is an important reason for improvements in hospital care and treatment in this period.

Hint

Look at this sample answer to Question 5. Refer back to the notes on page 71, then look to see how some of the points are used here.

Effective plan helps to keep answer clear, well structured and focused.

Including a judgement in the plan helps keep the whole answer focused.

Short introduction says what answer will discuss and gives clear judgement on the opinion in the statement.

Sticks to date range given in question.

Language used shows writing is analytical and giving a judgement.

Paragraph starts with a point focused on the question.

Shows detailed knowledge and understanding of a factor given in question.

Includes specific examples of accurate evidence.

Explains how the factor caused the change – the improvements in care and treatment – in the question, and links back to question.

Language clearly signposts second example will be discussed.

Uses own knowledge to discuss a factor not included in the question.

Detailed own knowledge used to explain impact of factor being discussed – Nightingale's work.

Use of key terms throughout shows strong understanding of topic.

Accurate spelling, punctuation and grammar throughout.

Makes links between factors.

Regularly links back to question.

Beginning of counter-argument clearly signposted.

Language shows analysis and gives a judgement about the statement in the question.

Language used shows writing is analytical – it is explaining why.

Accurate use of subject terminology.

Sticks to the dates given in the question.

Uses accurate subject knowledge as evidence – here, knowledge of aseptic conditions.

Gives a reason for judgement.

Another example of a way that Florence Nightingale's work is important is the effect she had on hygiene. Before 1850, conditions in hospitals were poor. Nightingale stressed the importance of the cleanliness of everything in the hospital, including wards, equipment, bed linen and nurses' uniforms. She did this because she believed in the miasma theory – that bad air caused disease – and thought hygiene and fresh air would help prevent people getting ill. Although the miasma theory was wrong, improving hygiene in hospitals helped prevent infection. Therefore, Nightingale's work in improving hygiene in hospitals like her work to improve nursing, played an important role in improving hospital treatment and care.

However, although I agree that Nightingale's work is important, I think the development of antiseptics is a more important reason for improvements in hospital care and treatment between c1700 and c1900. Joseph Lister was a surgeon at Glasgow Royal Infirmary and he noticed that about half of his patients died from infections caused during or after surgery. Lister found that carbolic acid reduced infections and invented a spray to clean wounds, surgical equipment and clothing. His wards became free of infection and he published his ideas so others could copy his methods. This led to further research which led to antiseptic conditions becoming common in hospitals by the 1890s. By 1900 most hospitals had moved towards aseptic conditions – where bacteria were not present at all. Instruments were steam cleaned, and doctors, surgeons and nurses wore face masks, gloves and gowns during surgery. Wards and operating theatres were thoroughly cleaned several times a day. This drastically reduced the risk of infection, so far fewer people died or became ill from infection in the first place. The development of antiseptics is therefore an extremely important reason for improvements in hospital treatment and care in this period and in my view it is more important than Nightingale's work.

Judgement made clear throughout answer.

Conclusion is clearly signposted.

In conclusion, Florence Nightingale's work is an important reason for the improvements in hospital treatment and care, especially her work in improving training for nurses and hygiene in hospitals. However, I do not agree that it is the most important reason. I think the development of antiseptics by Joseph Lister was more important because its consequences – the development of antiseptic and aseptic conditions – had a greater impact, making more advanced treatments and major surgery possible because the risk of infection had been reduced.

Conclusion gives clear, overall judgement.

Conclusion briefly compares factors discussed in answer.

Judgement is fully justified with reasons.

A very strong answer because...

In this analytical explanation, the student considers arguments for the statement in the question and arguments against it. Each point is supported with clear and accurate evidence, and the student explains why this supports or challenges the statement. The answer is also supported with relevant information from the student's own knowledge. The student reaches an overall judgement in the conclusion and gives reasons for their decision. Starting with a good plan has helped the student to organise their argument clearly and to stay focused on the question. Spelling, punctuation, grammar and use of specialist terminology are also accurate throughout.

Hint

Read the notes below, then look at the sample answer on page 76.

Hint

Remember – in the exam you only need to answer **either** Question 5 **or** Question 6.

Answer EITHER Question 5 OR Question 6.
Spelling, punctuation, grammar and use of specialist terminology will be assessed in this question.

6 'The development of penicillin is the most important breakthrough in the treatment of disease since c1800.'

How far do you agree? Explain your answer.

(16 marks plus 4 marks for SPaG and use of specialist terminology)

You may use the following in your answer:

- Alexander Fleming, Howard Florey and Ernst Chain
- high-tech treatments

You **must** also use information of your own.

Writing a good answer

Good answers will:

- give an analytical explanation which is tightly focused on the question throughout
- keep explanations clear and well organised throughout
- include information that is accurate, relevant and closely linked to the question
- show a wide range of knowledge and understanding of the topic
- reach an overall judgement which is fully justified
- use correct spelling, punctuation and grammar and specialist terms.

Relevant points that support the statement may include:

- Penicillin, which was discovered by Fleming and developed by Florey and Chain, prevented many deaths from infection in the Second World War.
- The development of penicillin led to the discovery and development of other antibiotics to treat more diseases.
- Scientists were eventually able to manufacture antibiotics rather than growing them, which was more efficient.
- Antibiotics are still an important part of medical treatment today and are able to treat many infections and diseases that, before the availability of antibiotics, were usually fatal.

Relevant points to counter the statement may include:

- Antibiotic resistance is developing so antibiotics are no longer effective in some cases.
- Charity and local government funding in the 19th and early 20th centuries widened access to hospital treatment.
- The establishment of the NHS in 1948 gave everyone access to healthcare and enabled the effective treatment of disease.
- High-tech treatments – such as keyhole surgery, robotic surgery, chemotherapy, radiotherapy and dialysis machines – are now used to treat diseases that were previously untreatable.

Q6: sample answer

Plan:

Support	Challenge
1. Fleming, Florey, Chain • Work led to mass prod. of penicillin • Penicillin used in WW2 to stop infection 2. Other antibiotics • Penicillin = discovery of more antibiotics • More infections treated + lives saved	1. More access to treatment • C19th and early C20th = local gov and charities funded hospitals • NHS 1948 – treatment for all 2. High-tech treatments • Dialysis machines, chemotherapy – new conditions treated • Better surgery, e.g. micro instruments + cameras
Judgement: Agree – penicillin still used today + millions of deaths prevented	

I agree that the most important breakthrough in the treatment of disease since c1800 is the development of penicillin. This is because it led to the development of more antibiotics which meant many diseases and infections that previously killed people could be treated. There were other important breakthroughs such as increased access to treatment because of increased government funding and the development of high-tech treatments but these did not have as much impact as antibiotics.

The development of penicillin had a significant impact on treating and curing some diseases and infections. In 1928, Alexander Fleming noticed that penicillin mould killed bacteria, then from 1939 Howard Florey and Ernst Chain continued Fleming's work and found that penicillin was effective at killing infections. Mass production of penicillin began in 1942, and as a result many soldiers wounded during the Second World War were cured of infection. Penicillin also began to be used to treat some diseases and wound infections in the general population. It was an important breakthrough because it saved thousands of lives. Its importance as a breakthrough in treating disease is supported by the fact that penicillin is still commonly used today.

Hint

Look at this sample answer to Question 6. Refer back to the notes on page 75, then look to see how some of the points are used here.

Effective plan helps to keep answer clear, well structured and focused.

Introduction starts with a clear judgement on the opinion in the statement.

Introduces the other factors that will be discussed.

Begins with a clear focus on the main factor in the statement.

Shows detailed knowledge and understanding of topic.

Language used shows writing is analytical – it is explaining why.

Includes specific and accurate evidence.

Explains why the factor was important.

Links back to the question.

Language clearly signposts that second example will be discussed.

Accurate spelling, punctuation and grammar throughout.

Makes links between factors.

Sticks to date range given in question.

Language used shows writing is analytical and gives a judgement.

Regularly links back to question.

Beginning of counter-argument clearly signposted.

Language shows analysis and gives a judgement about the statement in the question.

Uses own knowledge to discuss a factor not included in the question.

Detailed own knowledge used to explain impact of factor being discussed – increased access to treatment.

Uses accurate subject knowledge as evidence.

Another reason why the development of penicillin was an important breakthrough in the treatment of disease is because the success of penicillin led to more antibiotics. Throughout the 1940s, 1950s and 1960s, scientists carried out further work on moulds and discovered more antibiotics which treated more diseases and infections. Antibiotics have had an absolutely massive impact on medicine as they have saved the lives of millions of people and continue to save lives today. Therefore, I agree that the development of penicillin is the most important breakthrough in the treatment of disease since c1800.

However, although I agree with the viewpoint in the statement, there have been other important breakthroughs since c1800. One example is the increase in access to treatment that is available. In the 18th century there were only a few hospitals but throughout the 19th and early 20th centuries, local government and charities opened more hospitals and paid for people's treatment in them. The major breakthrough was the government setting up the National Health Service in 1948. This led to more hospitals being built and medical care being available to everyone. This had a huge impact on the treatment of disease as people no longer had to pay for treatment. This was an important breakthrough, though it did not affect the actual treatments available so I do not think it was as much of a breakthrough as the development of penicillin.

Explains why this factor was important.

Uses the second bullet point given in the question to add to counter-argument.

High-tech treatments are another important breakthrough in the treatment of disease since c1800. Science and technology have helped create many machines, such as dialysis machines to treat kidney disease and micro instruments and cameras to carry out keyhole surgery, and new treatments such as radiotherapy and chemotherapy to treat cancer. As a result, it is now possible to successfully treat more conditions and diseases than before. Therefore, high-tech treatments are an important breakthrough in the treatment of disease and they are still used today.

Accurate use of subject terminology and spelled correctly.

Frequent use of key terms shows strong topic knowledge.

Overall, I agree with the statement. There have been many important breakthroughs in the treatment of disease since c1800, such as improved access to treatment as a result of the creation of the NHS and the ability to treat conditions for the first time thanks to the development of high-tech treatments. However, I think these are less important than the development of penicillin, which was the first antibiotic. Antibiotics are a 'miracle' cure for many types of disease and infection and are continuing to save millions of lives. Consequently, I agree that the development of penicillin is the most important breakthrough in the treatment of disease since c1800.

Conclusion summarises argument and comes to an overall judgement.

Compares factors and gives reasons for judgement.

reason for judgement.

A very strong swer because...

clear judgement is given in the introduction, which is then followed throughout the answer. The analysis covers guments for and against the statement in the question, and the counter-argument is clearly signposted. e student uses their own knowledge to support their argument, and points are backed up with relevant and curate evidence. The conclusion offers an overall judgement that is fully justified with reasons. The plan the udent made helped them to produce an answer that is well organised throughout. Spelling, punctuation, ammar and use of specialist terminology are also accurate.

Answers

Where an exemplar answer is given, this is not necessarily the only correct response. In most cases there is a range of responses that can gain full marks.

KNOWLEDGE BOOSTER

1. The Middle Ages

1 A. True

B. True

C. False – the Church discouraged people from challenging its ideas.

D. False – Galen was not a Christian.

E. True

F. True

2

Blood	Spring	Air	Hot and wet
Yellow bile	Summer	Fire	Hot and dry
Black bile	Autumn	Earth	Cold and dry
Phlegm	Winter	Water	Cold and wet

3 **(a)** Hippocrates

(b) Galen

4 Theory of Opposites

5 The Hippocratic Oath

6 Bleeding; purging

7 Miasma was 'bad air' that came from rotting organic matter. People thought that the bad air caused disease.

2. The Middle Ages

8

	Training	Costs	Examples of services they provided
Physicians	University	Expensive	Any two from: • Diagnosing illnesses and treatments • Sending patients to apothecaries or barber surgeons • Carrying out some treatments
Apothecaries	Some	Fairly cheap	Any two from: • Diagnosing illnesses and treatments • Mixing medicines to treat illness • Carrying out physicians' instructions
Barber surgeons	None	Fairly cheap	Any two from: • Bleeding • Pulling teeth out • Lancing boils • Cutting hair • Amputating limbs

9 Aii; Biii; Ci

10 One from:

- A place for travellers to stay
- Recuperation

(In addition, some hospitals for infectious diseases appeared towards the end of the Middle Ages.)

11 Praying and fasting

Plus at least three from:

- Clearing the streets
- Flagellation
- Not letting unknown people enter the town/village
- Lighting fires
- Trying to keep the sick away from the well

3. The Renaissance

1 Any two from:

- That God was displeased or testing people
- Supernatural ideas
- Astrology
- Miasma
- Theory of the Four Humours

2 During the Renaissance, people challenged old ideas. This included religious ideas. Most people still believed in God but the authority of the Church declined. Fewer people accepted that God caused disease and people started to look for new, rational ideas instead. Gradually there was a new scientific approach to diagnosing illness.

3 **(a)** B

(b) C

(c) A

4. The Renaissance

4 B

5 William Harvey proved that Vesalius was right and that blood flowed towards the heart. This proved that Galen was wrong. Harvey discovered that blood was pumped around the body by the heart. He was a royal physician so his work was widely read. By 1700 it was being taught in medical schools. His methods of observation and dissection were copied by others who wanted to find out more.

6

Similarities	Differences
• Sufferers and their families were quarantined Plus any two from: • Praying and fasting • Clearing up the streets • Carrying herbs and spices to avoid 'bad air' • Herbal remedies	• Great Plague: Sufferers were wrapped up and put by fires to try to sweat disease out Plus any two from: • Great Plague: Theory of transference – people tried to 'transfer' disease to something else (especially birds) • Black Death: Unknown people were not allowed into town • Great Plague: Large gatherings were banned • Great Plague: Local councils were heavily involved in trying to stop the spread

5. 18th and 19th centuries

1 1G; 2C; 3A; 4F; 5E; 6B; 7H; 8D

2 She helped make nursing a more respectable job for women.

Plus at least two from:

- She helped improve hospital cleanliness, which reduced infection and lowered death rates
- She helped improve training for nurses
- She set up her own training school for nurses and midwives
- She helped improve hospital organisation
- She influenced the design of hospitals as she emphasised fresh air and hygiene
- Nurses were given a more important role in patient care
- Her work was widely publicised

3 James Simpson discovered that chloroform was an effective anaesthetic. Joseph Lister discovered that carbolic spray was an effective antiseptic. He inspired others to search for methods to prevent infection which led to aseptic conditions for surgery by 1900.

6. 18th and 19th centuries

4 A. False – Jenner never worked out why the vaccination was effective.

B. False – the Royal Society refused to publish Jenner's ideas.

C. True

D. False – vaccination was popular around the world but took time to be accepted in Britain.

E. False – the link between cowpox and smallpox was unique so it didn't lead to other vaccinations.

F. False – there was widespread opposition to Jenner's ideas.

5 **(a)** A

(b) C

(c) C

(d) A

(e) C

(f) C

7. Modern Britain

1 **(a)** Watson and Crick

(b) Rosalind Franklin (working with Maurice Wilkins)

(c) Double helix

(d) Human Genome Project

2 Aii; Bi; Ciii

3

Technology used in diagnosis since 1900	Technology used in treatment since 1900
• MRI, CT and ultrasound scans Plus any two from: • X-rays • Microscopes • Endoscopes • Blood pressure monitors • Blood sugar monitors • Robots and cameras used in surgery • Hypodermic needles	• Dialysis machines Plus any two from: • Incubators • Prosthetic limbs • Pacemakers • Insulin pumps • Robots and cameras used in surgery • Hypodermic needles

4 Since the creation of the NHS in 1948, the UK government has funded more medical research to find more ways to prevent disease. It also funds vaccinations to prevent people contracting diseases such as polio and tetanus/measles. There have been laws to improve health and safety at work and reduce pollution. The government has also funded lifestyle campaigns to raise awareness of dangers to health and encourage healthy behaviour.

8. Modern Britain

5 **(a)** Magic bullet

(b) Antibiotic

(c) Syphilis

(d) Penicillin

(e) Blood poisoning/pneumonia/scarlet fever/ meningitis

6 **1928** Alexander Fleming discovers that mould kills bacteria.

1929 Fleming published his research but had no funding to continue his research.

1939 Howard Florey and Ernst Chain continue Fleming's research into penicillin.

1940 Florey and Chain prove that penicillin effectively kills infection in mice.

1941 US drug companies agree to fund Florey and Chain's research after UK companies would not. Florey and Chain prove that penicillin effectively kills infection in humans.

1942 American government finances mass production of penicillin in the USA.

1943 British drug companies begin mass production of penicillin.

7 Any two from:
- Banning advertising for cigarettes
- High tax on tobacco products to make smoking expensive
- Raising the legal age for buying tobacco products
- Educating people about risks of smoking
- Shops not allowed to publicly display cigarettes or tobacco
- Smoking banned in public places from 2007 in England
- Cigarette packaging has to display warnings of the dangers of smoking

9. The Western Front

1 **(a)** First Battle of Ypres: Oct–Nov 1914

(b) Battle on Hill 60: April 1915

(c) Second Battle of Ypres: April–May 1915

(d) The Somme: July–Nov 1916

(e) Arras: April–May 1917

(f) Third Battle of Ypres: July–Nov 1917

(g) Cambrai: Nov–Dec 1917

2 Any two from:
- Reserve trench
- Artillery emplacements
- Dugouts
- Support trench
- Frontline trench

3

	Cause	Symptoms	Example of prevention method
Trench fever	Lice – flourished in overcrowded and dirty trenches	Flu-like fever, which could keep recurring once contracted	In 1918 troops were deloused
Trench foot	Muddy, waterlogged trenches	Infected feet, which could lead to gangrene	For example: • Whale oil and spare socks to protect feet • Pumps used to drain water from trenches • Duckboards added to trenches so troops could get their feet out of water

4 **(a)** High-explosive shells and shrapnel

(b) Tetanus; gas gangrene

(c) Any two from:
- Blindness
- Coughing
- Burns

10. The Western Front

5 Royal Army Medical Corps (RAMC) and First Aid Nursing Yeomanry (FANY)

6 Immediate first aid

7 Several miles from the front line

8

	Situation pre-1914	Situation during war	Impact of war: advances made
Preventing and dealing with infection	Antiseptic, then aseptic surgery was established to prevent infection during surgery and other procedures	• Wounds infected before surgery • Antiseptic/aseptic surgery impossible in dressing stations and casualty clearing stations	• Surgeons used chemical sprays on wounds (didn't work on gas gangrene) • Carrel-Dakin method developed by 1917 – cleansed wound by moving sterilised salt solution through the wound using tubes • Surgery advanced and use of x-rays meant infected tissue as well as all traces of the bullet and shrapnel were removed
X-rays	X-ray machines were developed in the late 19th century but were large and very heavy	Huge numbers of bullet and shrapnel injuries meant x-ray machines were essential for effective surgery	• X-ray machines common in base hospitals from 1914 • Mobile machines developed and numbers increased so they could be used in casualty clearing stations and even dressing stations – saved many lives
Blood loss	• Human-to-human blood transfusions tried but often unsuccessful • Blood groups discovered in 1901	Blood loss a huge problem and caused many deaths	• Blood transfusions used from 1915 but limited as blood couldn't be stored • Methods found which preserved blood for longer – first 'blood depot' used at Cambrai, 1917

Notes

Notes

Notes